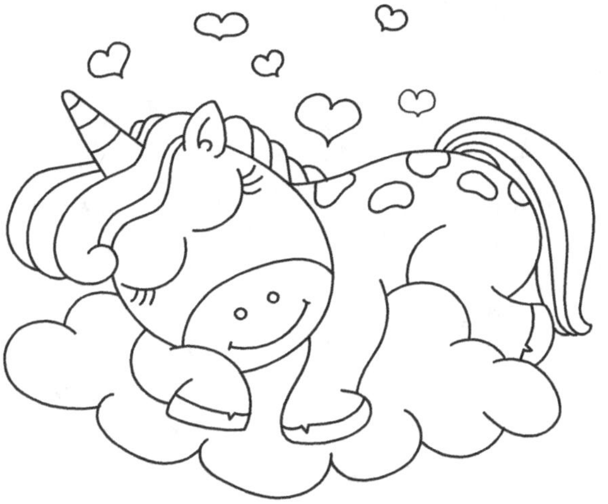

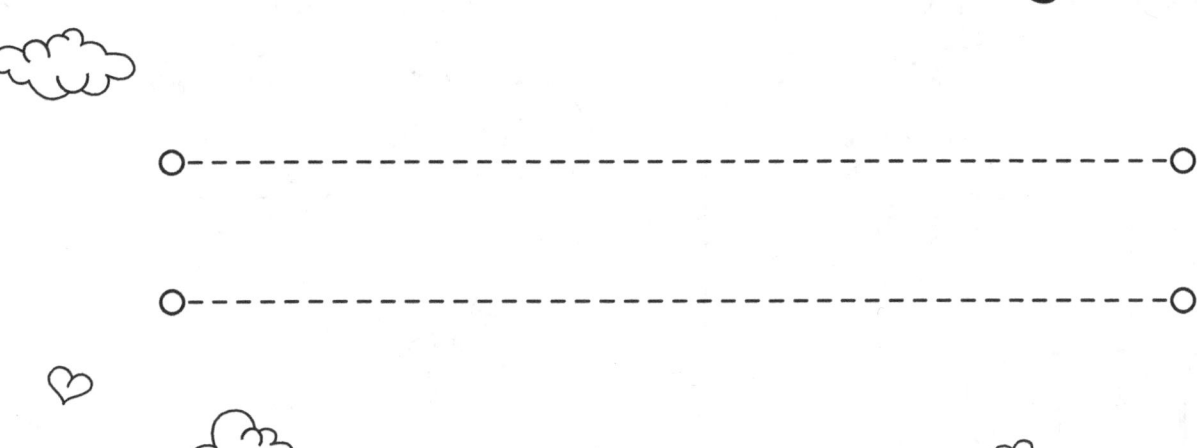

This Fun Art Book Belongs To:

○- ○

○- ○

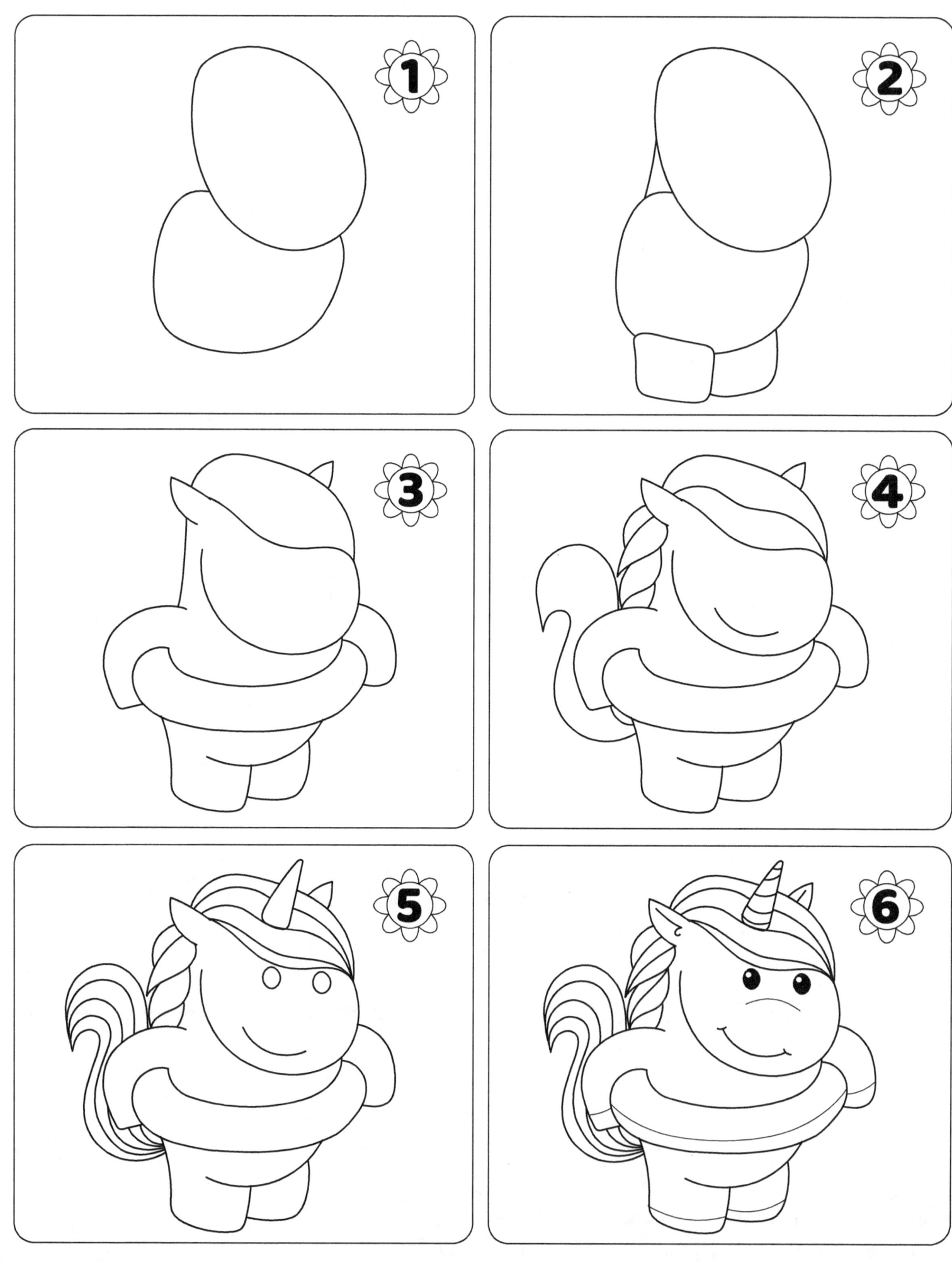

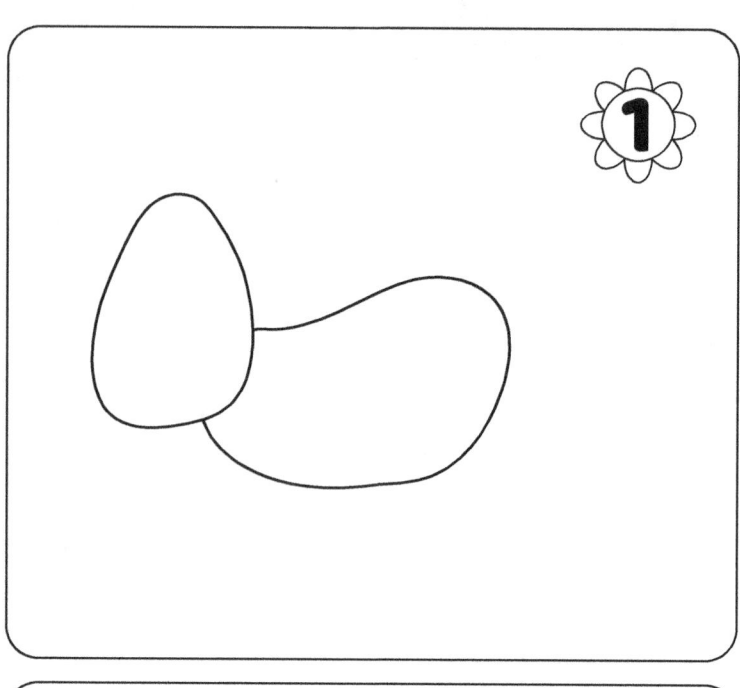

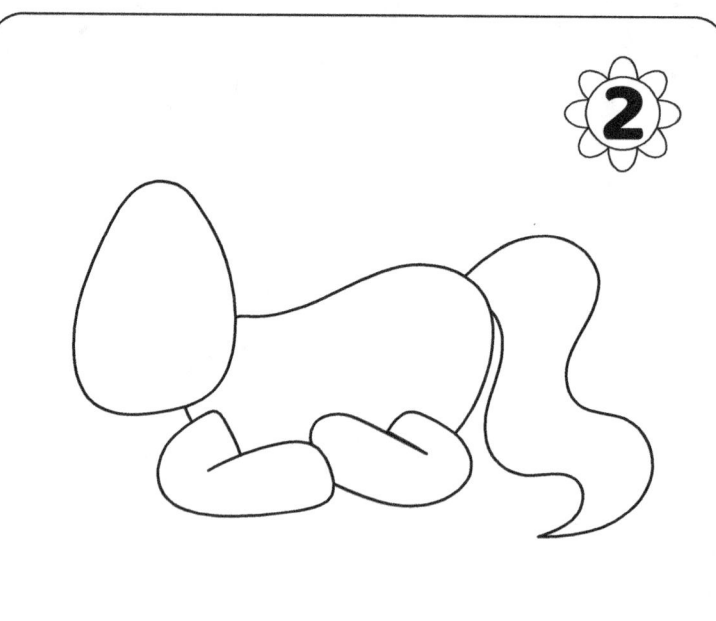

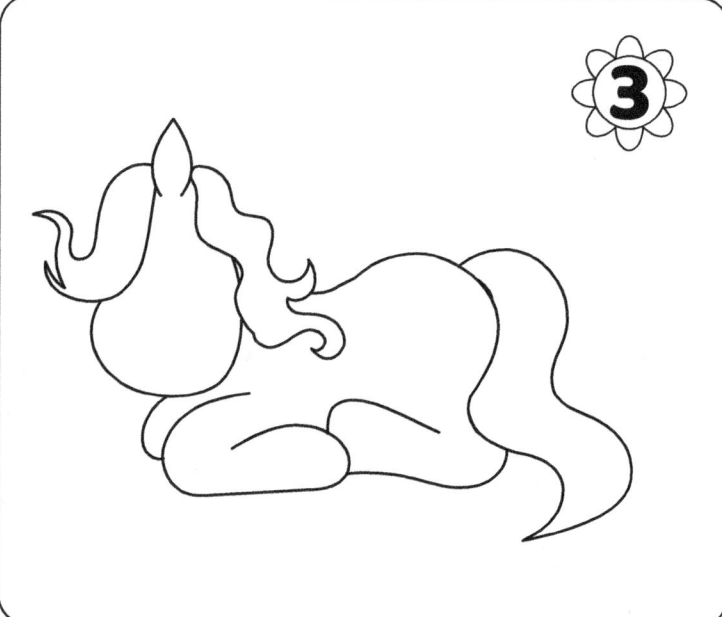

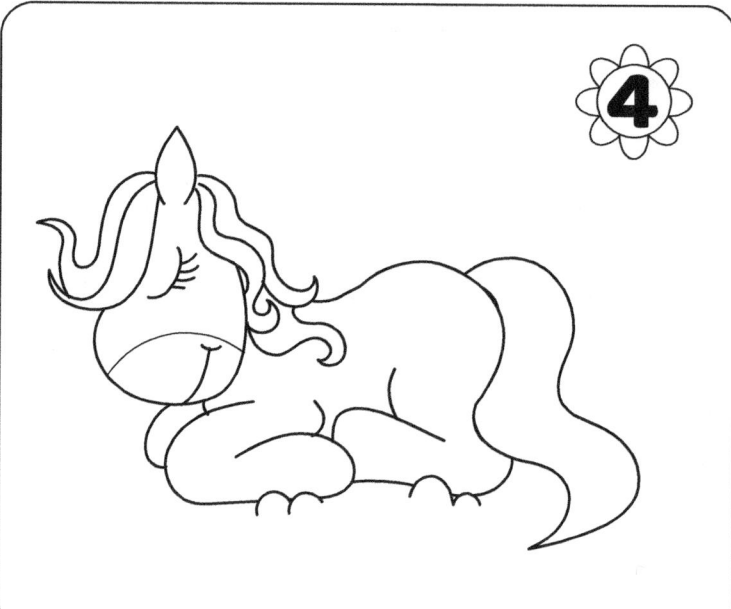

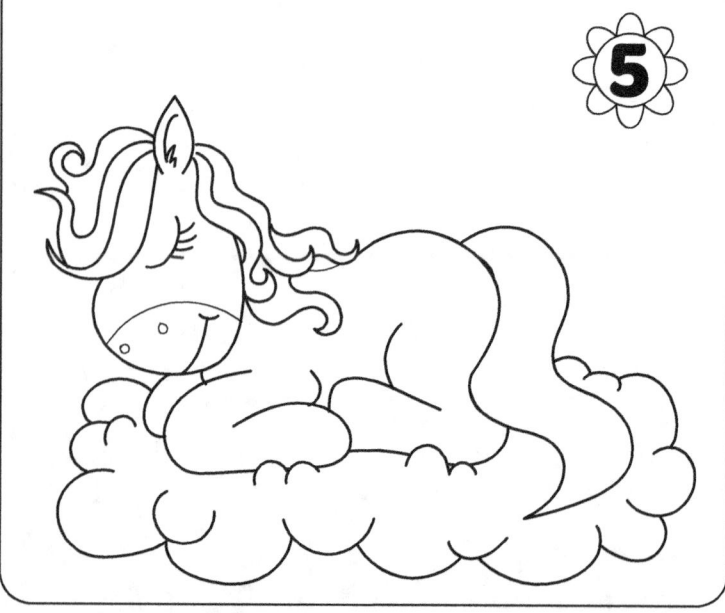

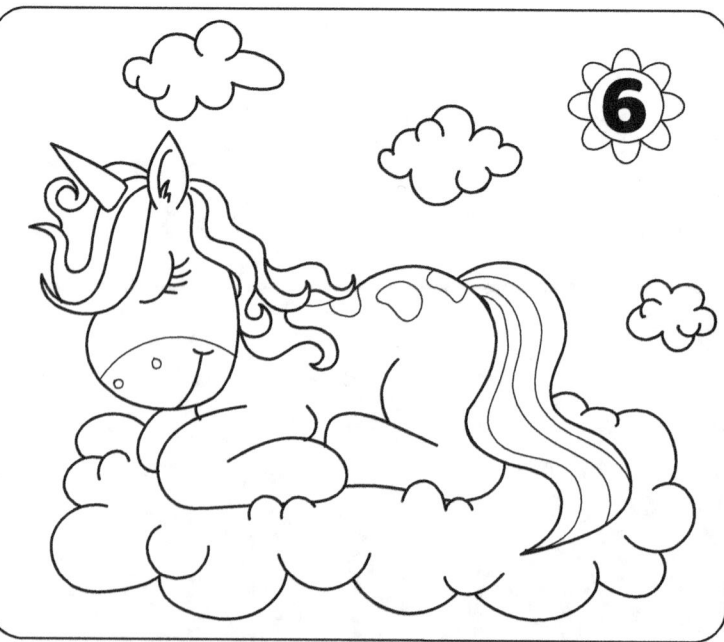

You Give It A Try!

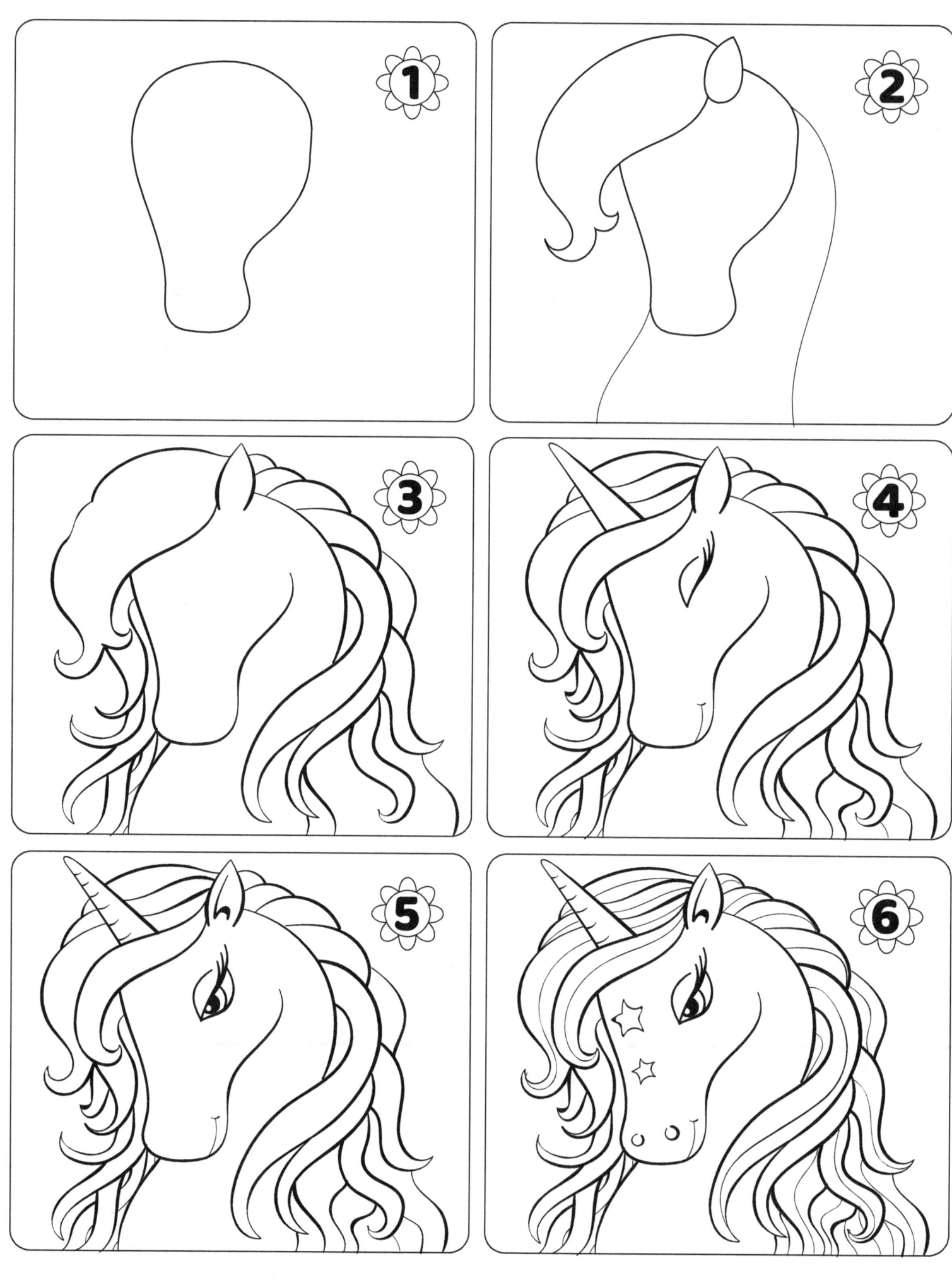

You Give It A Try!

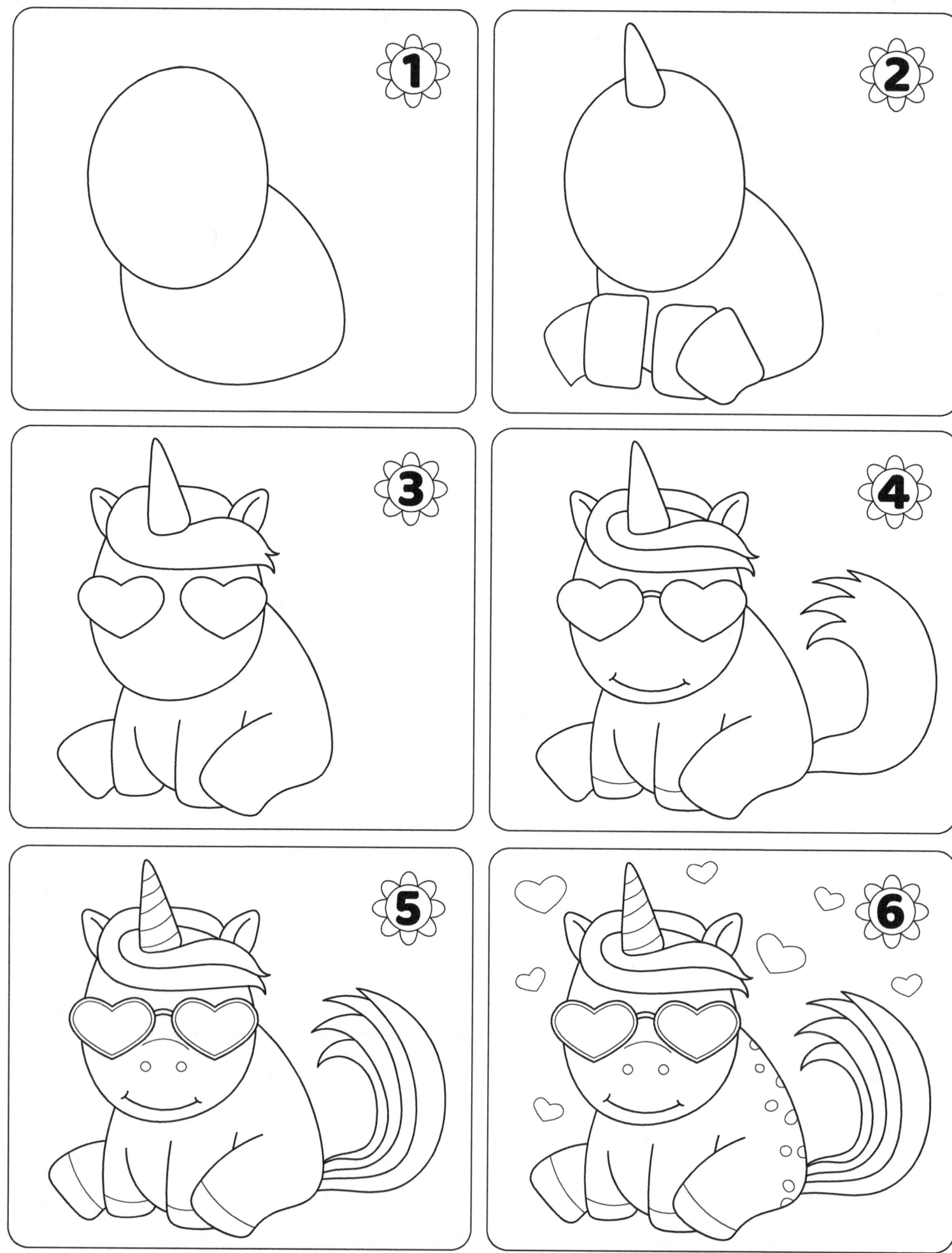

You Give It A Try!

You Give It A Try!

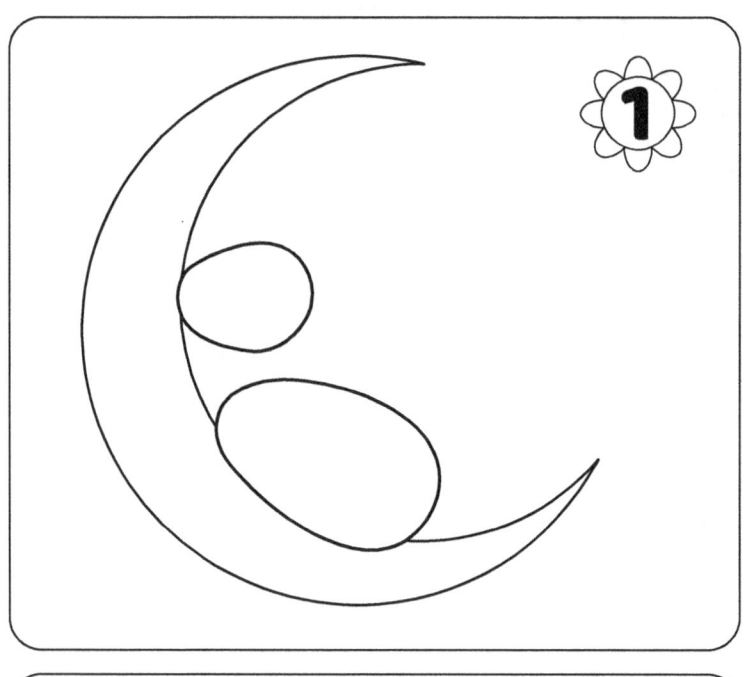

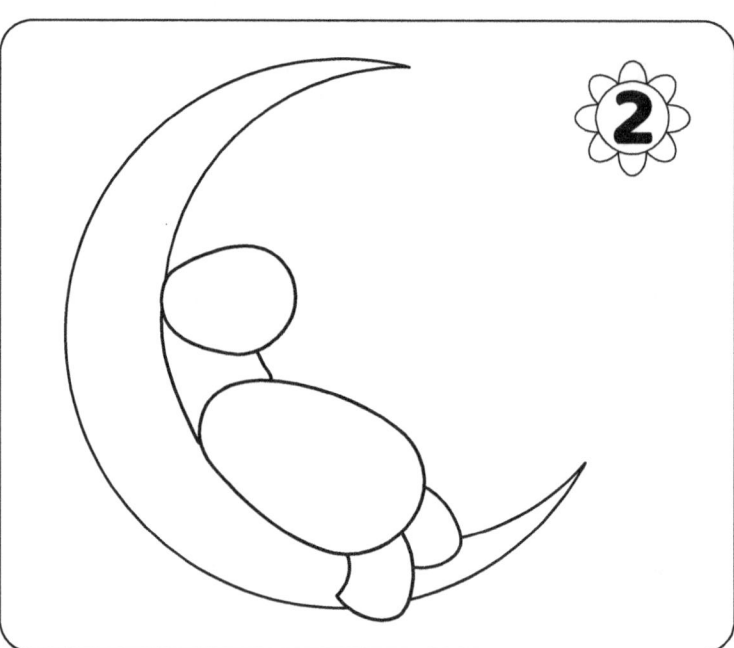

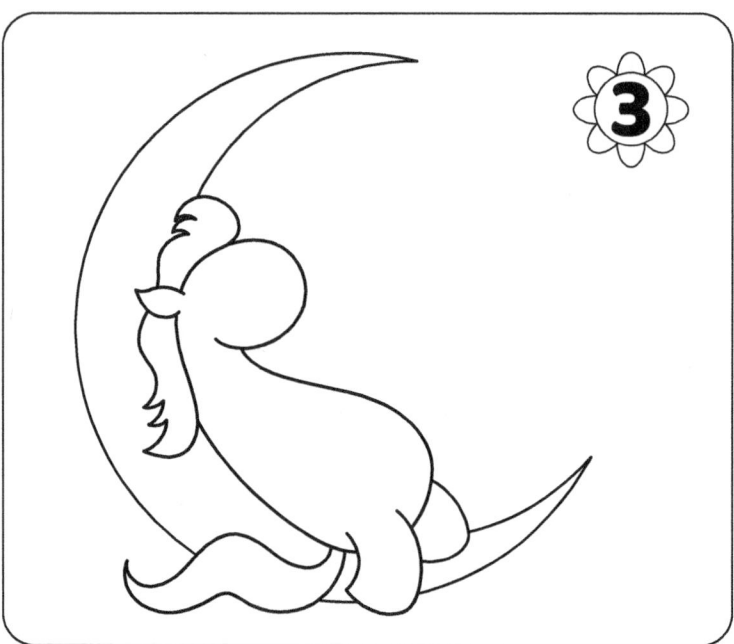

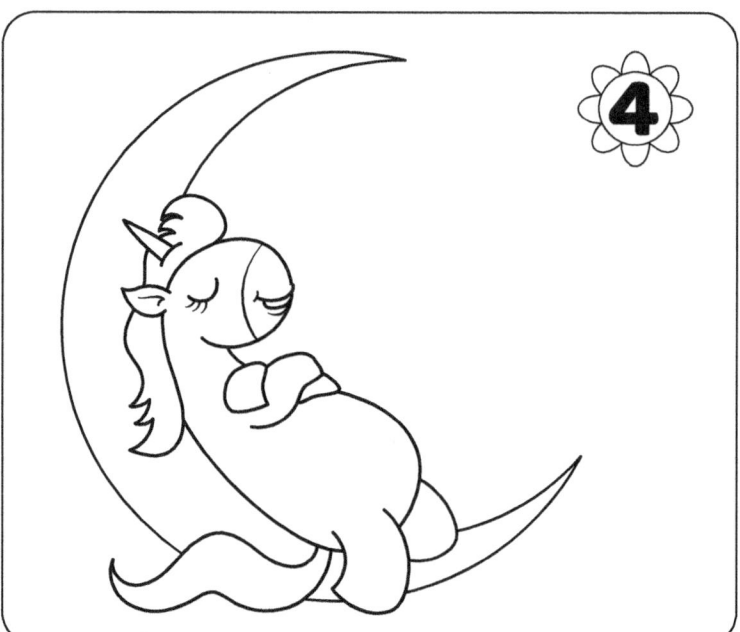

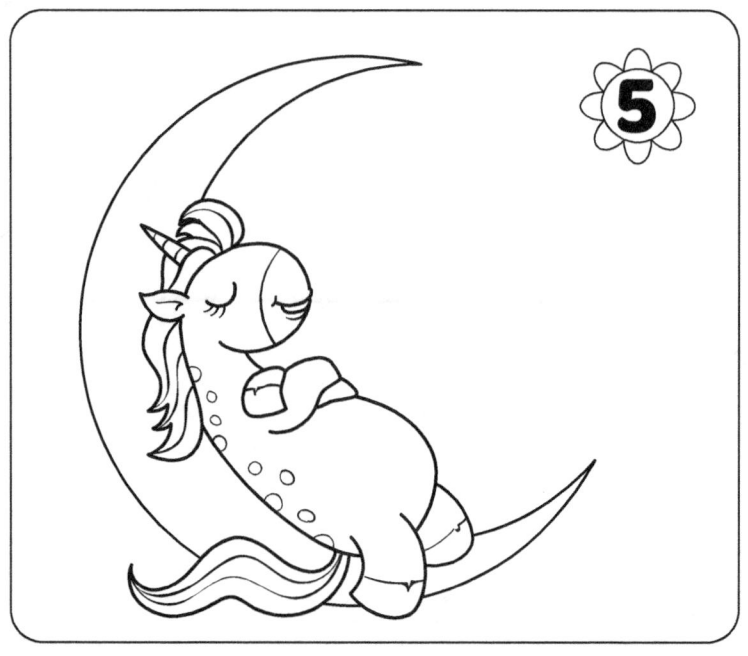

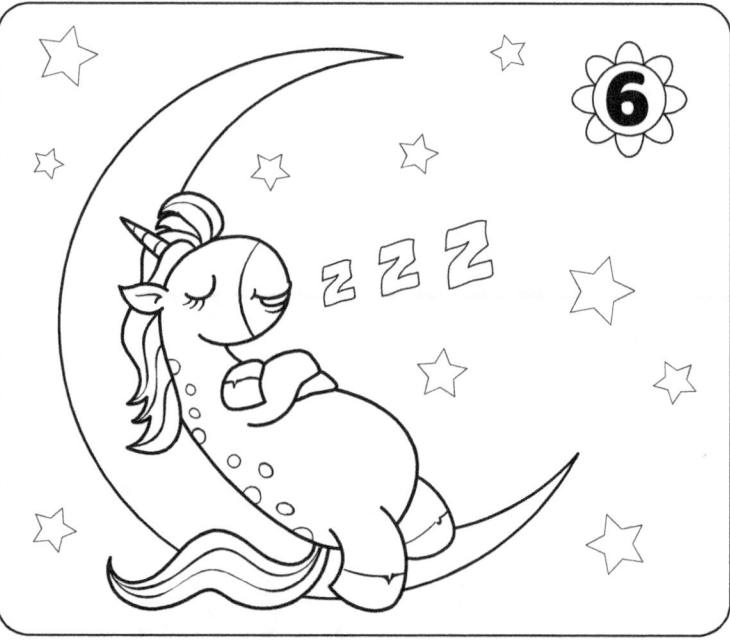

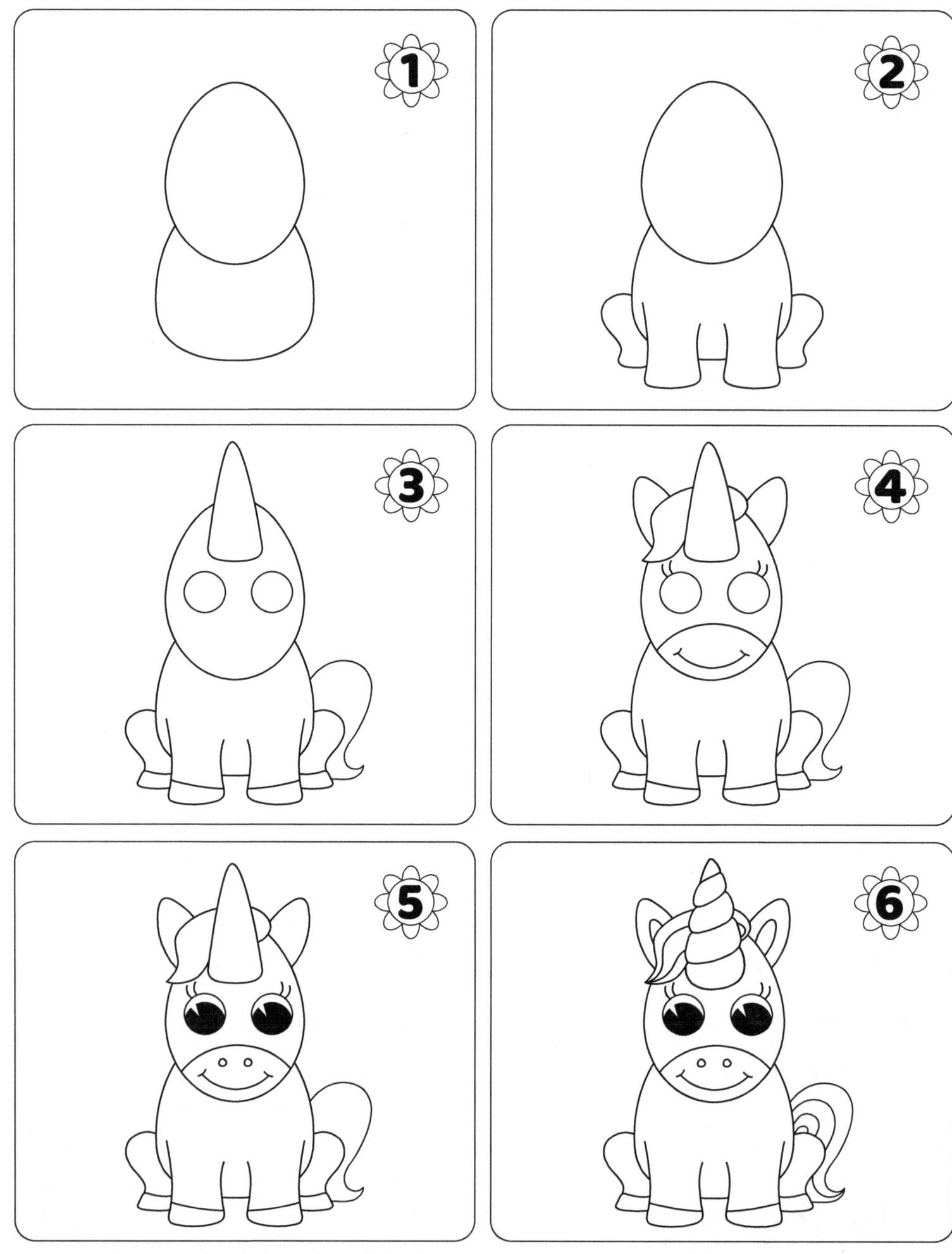

You Give It A Try!

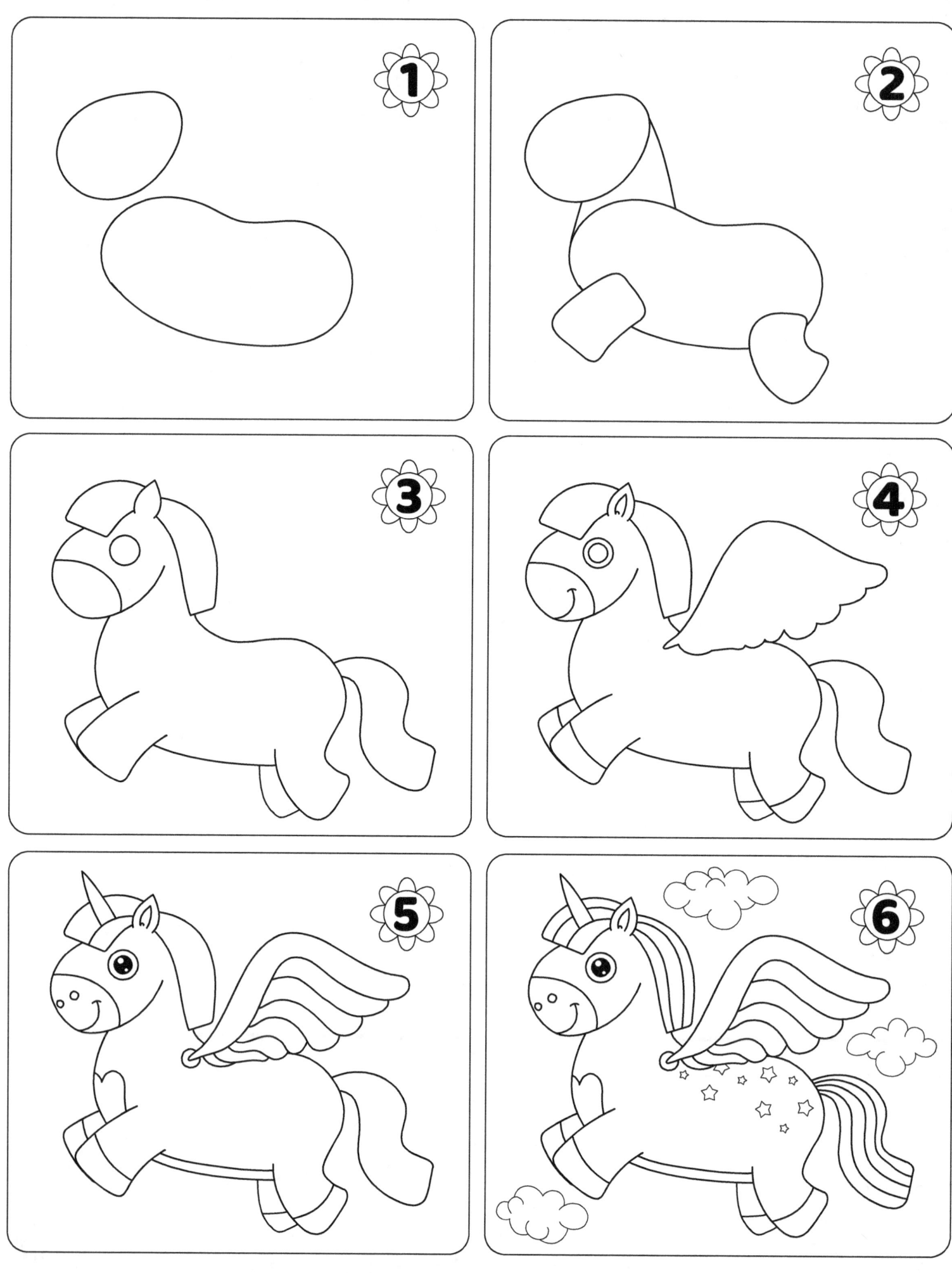

You Give It A Try!

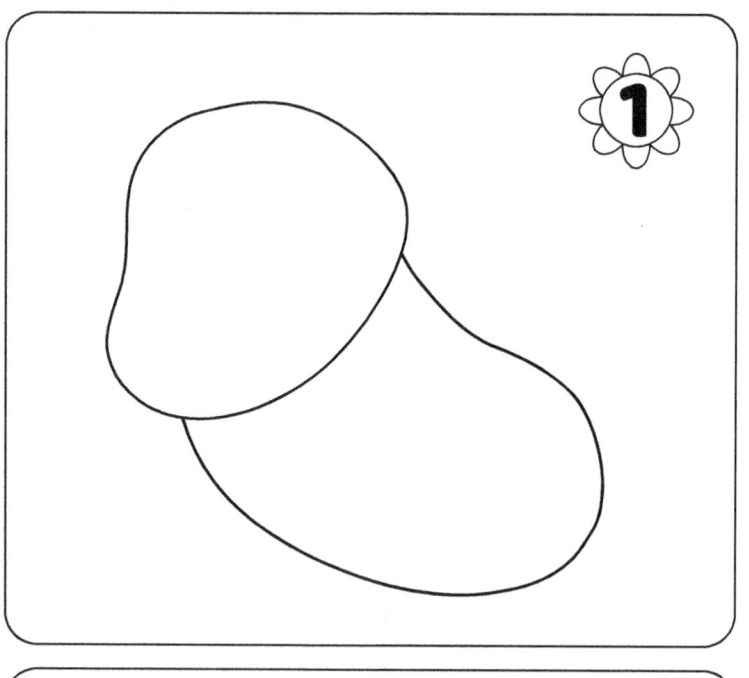

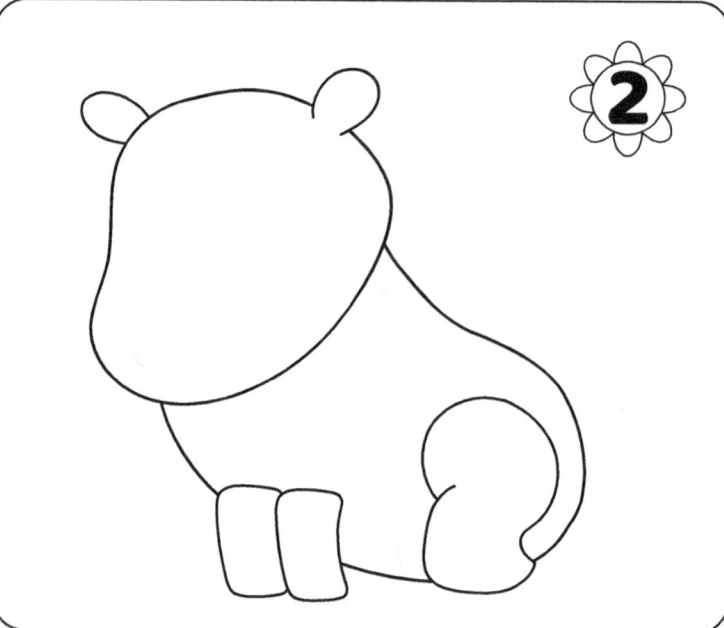

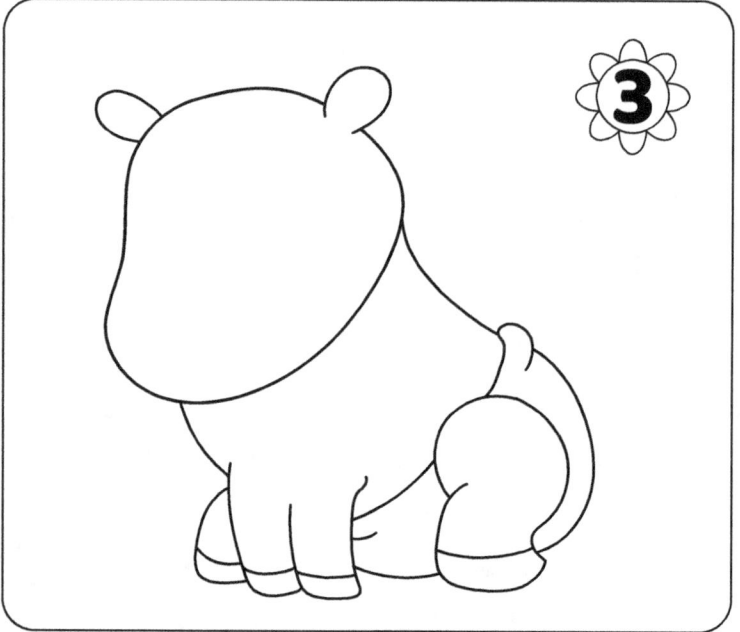

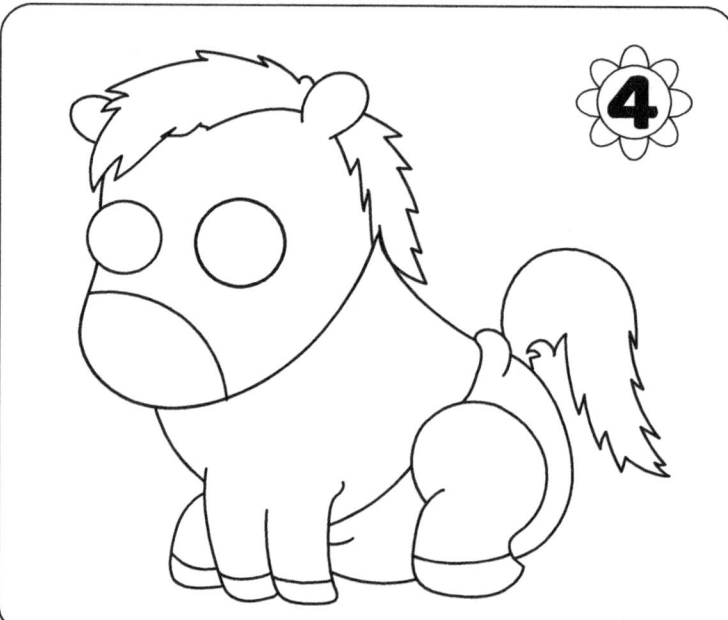

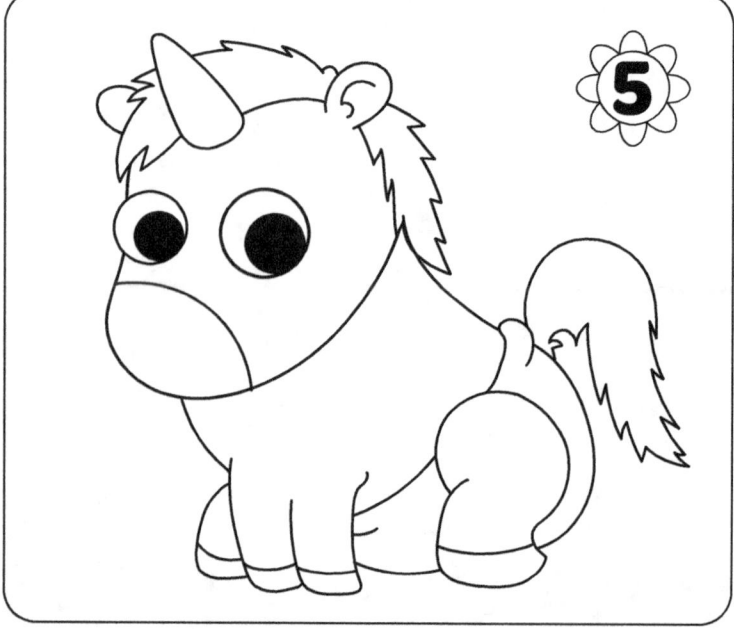

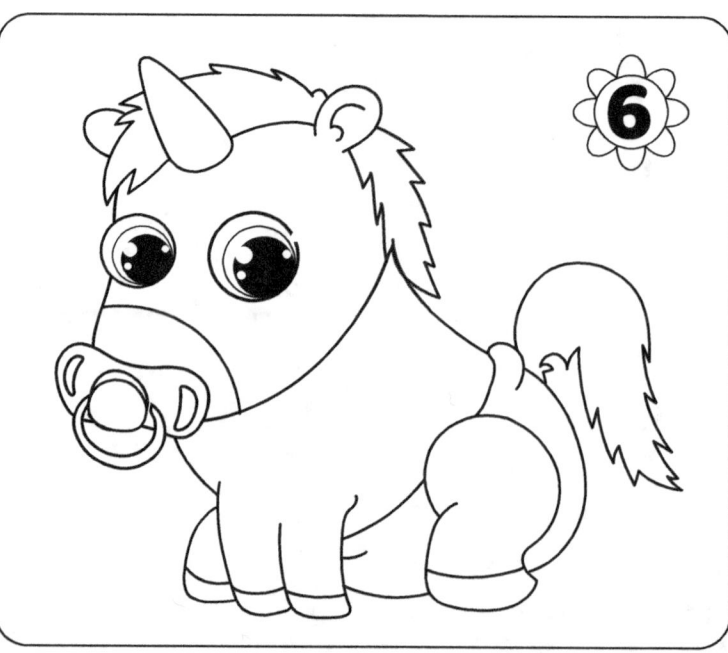

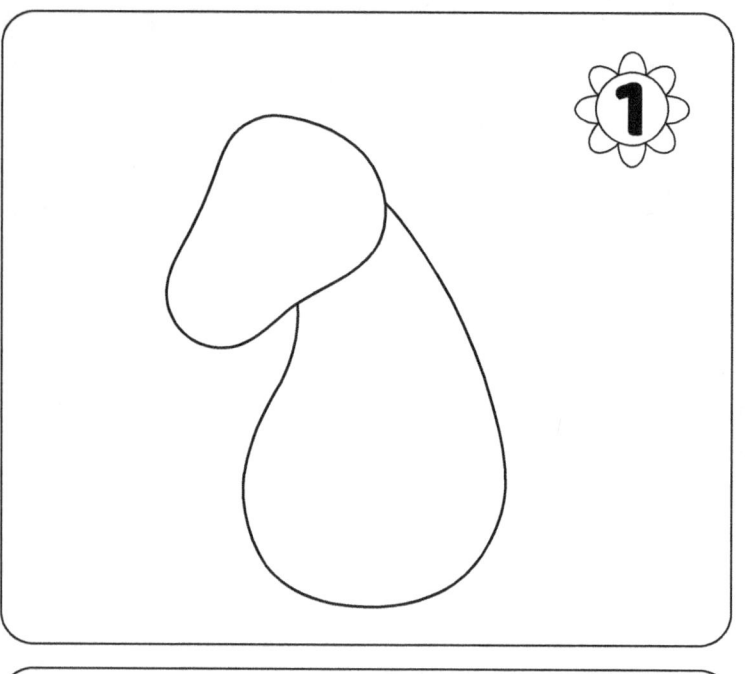

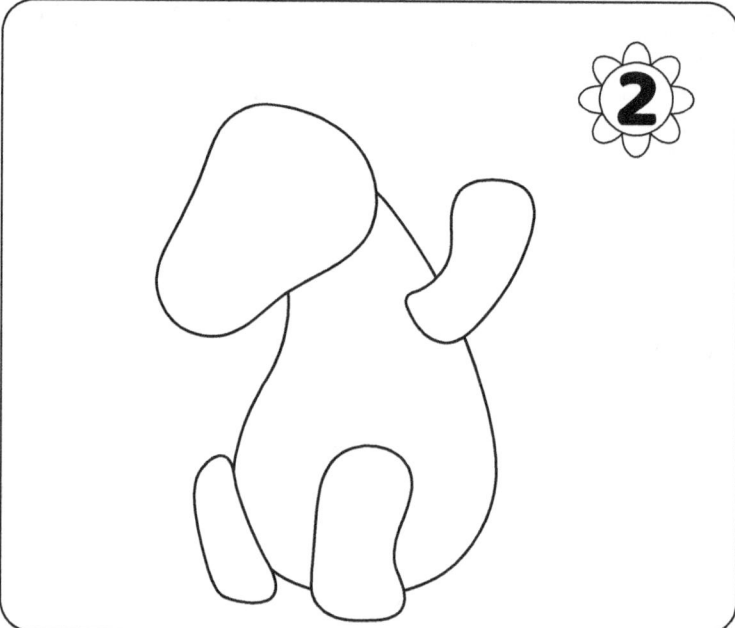

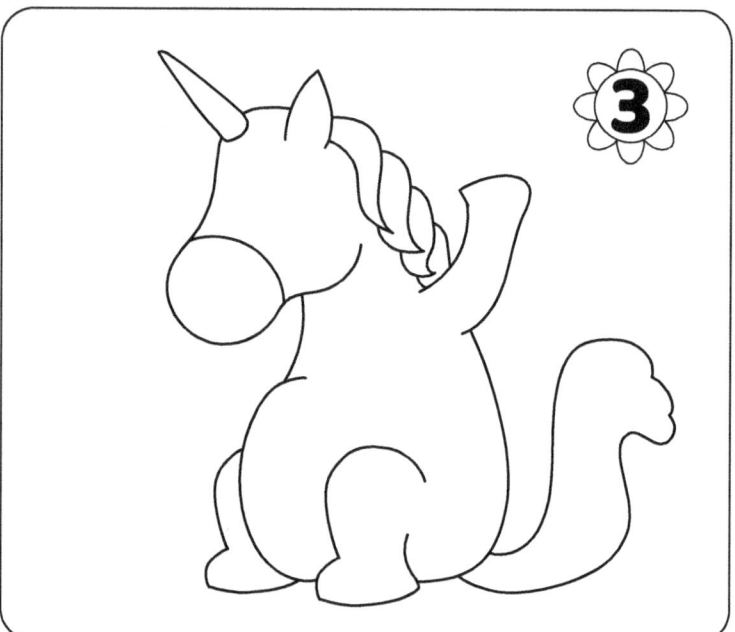

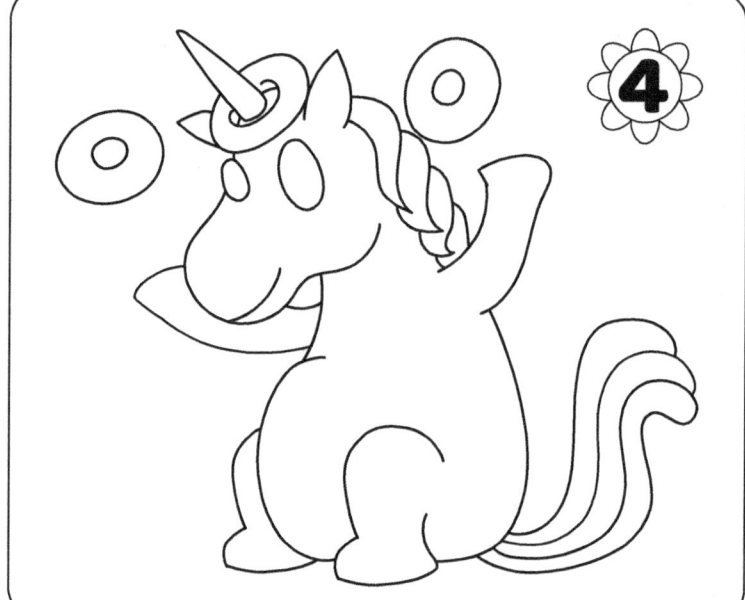

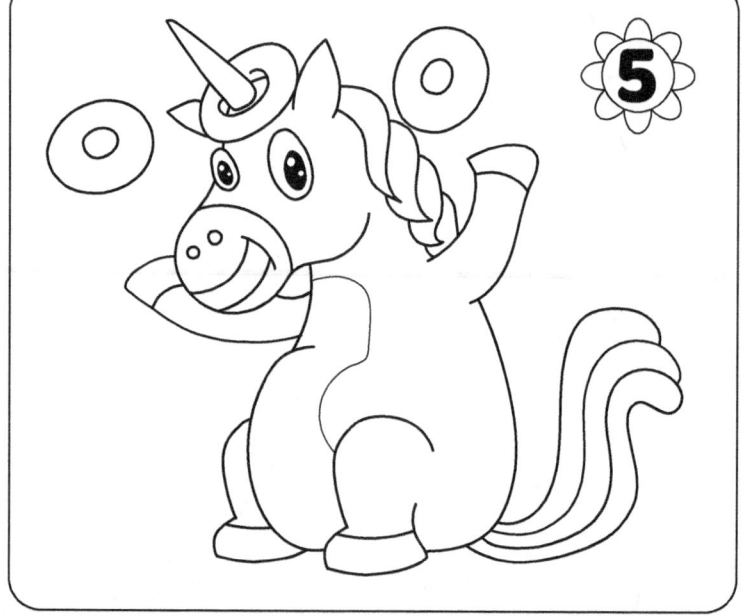

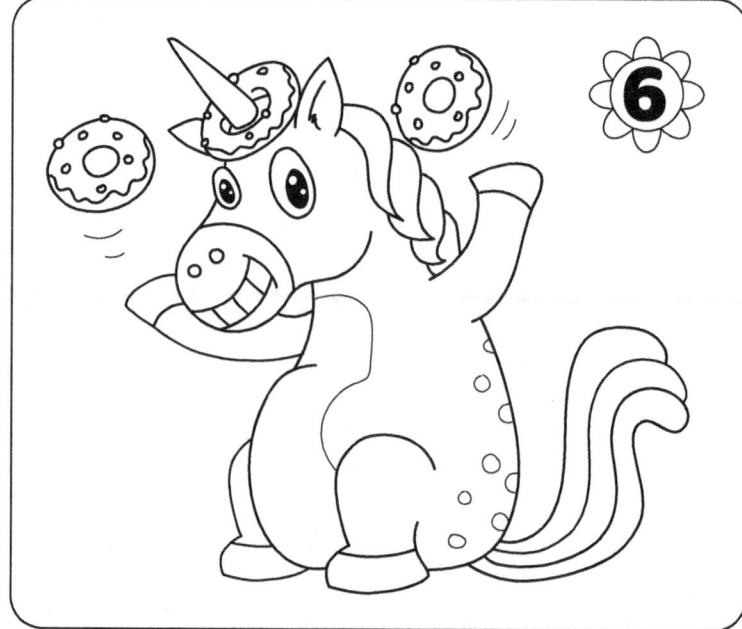

You Give It A Try!

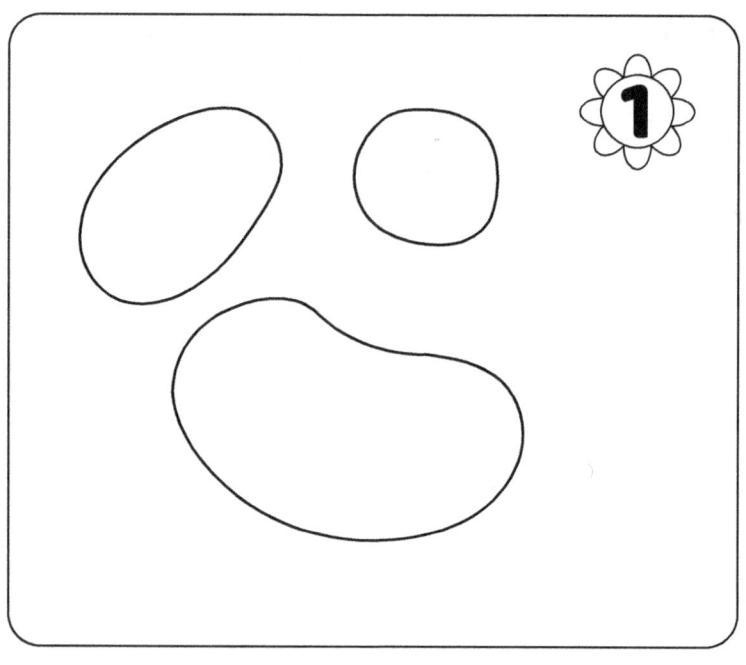

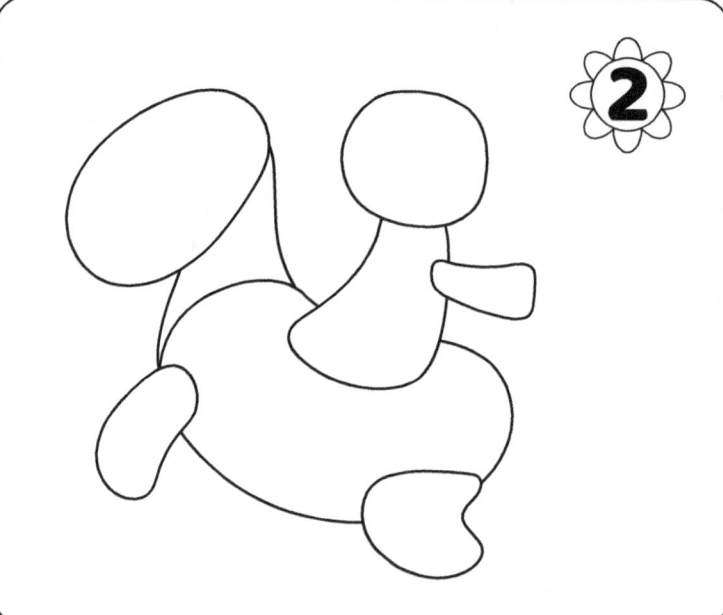

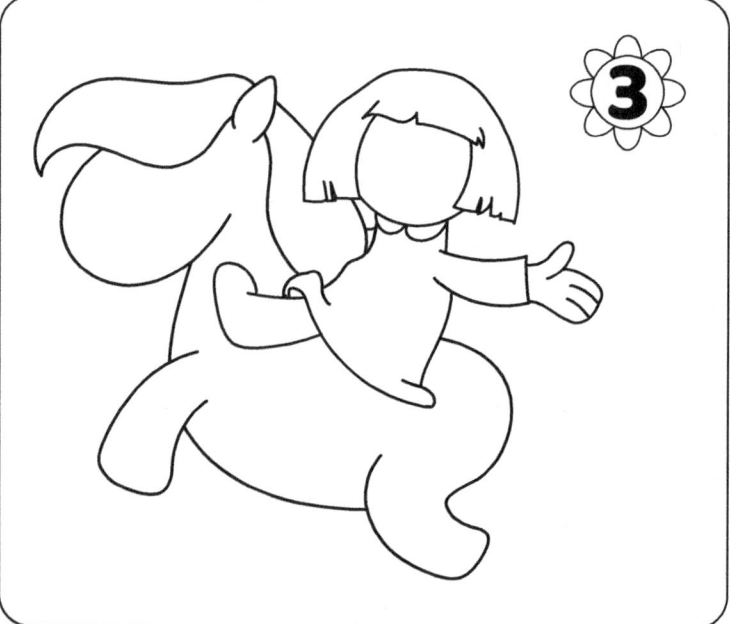

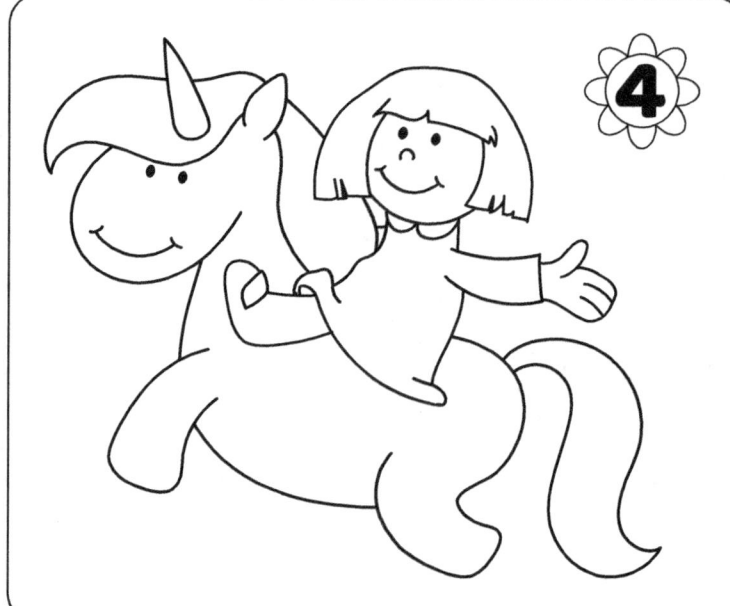

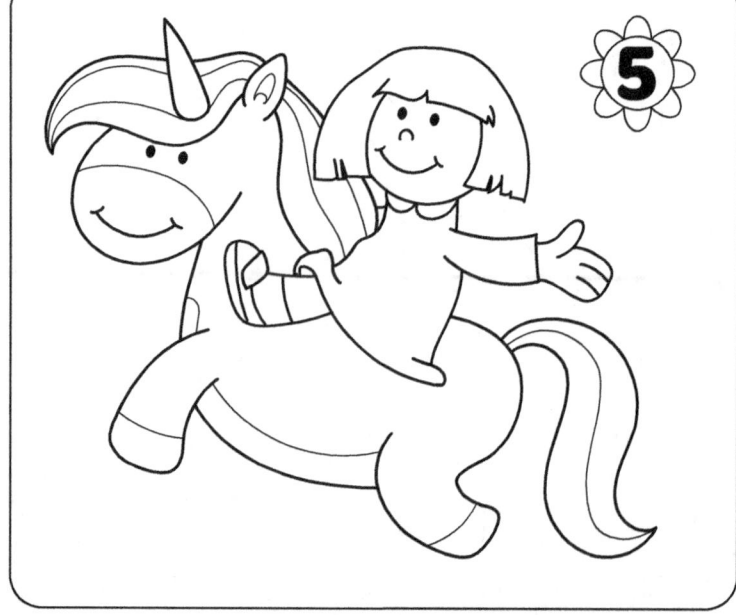

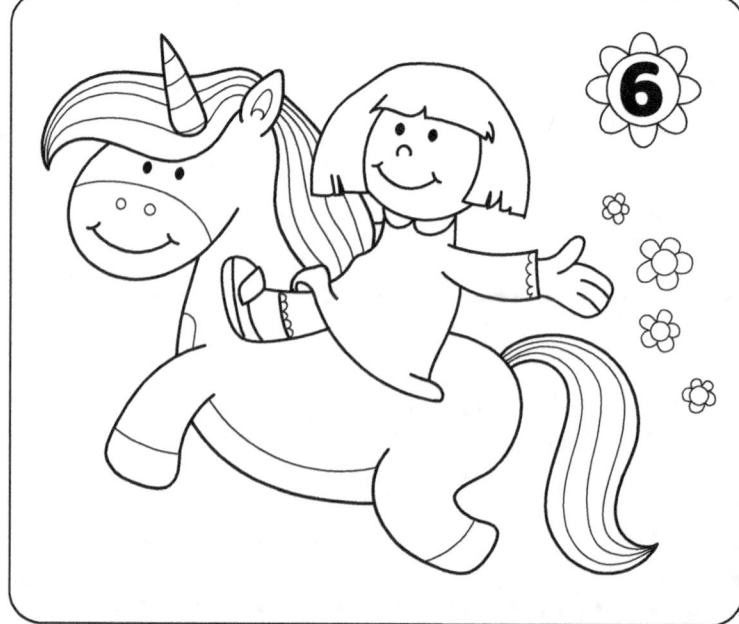

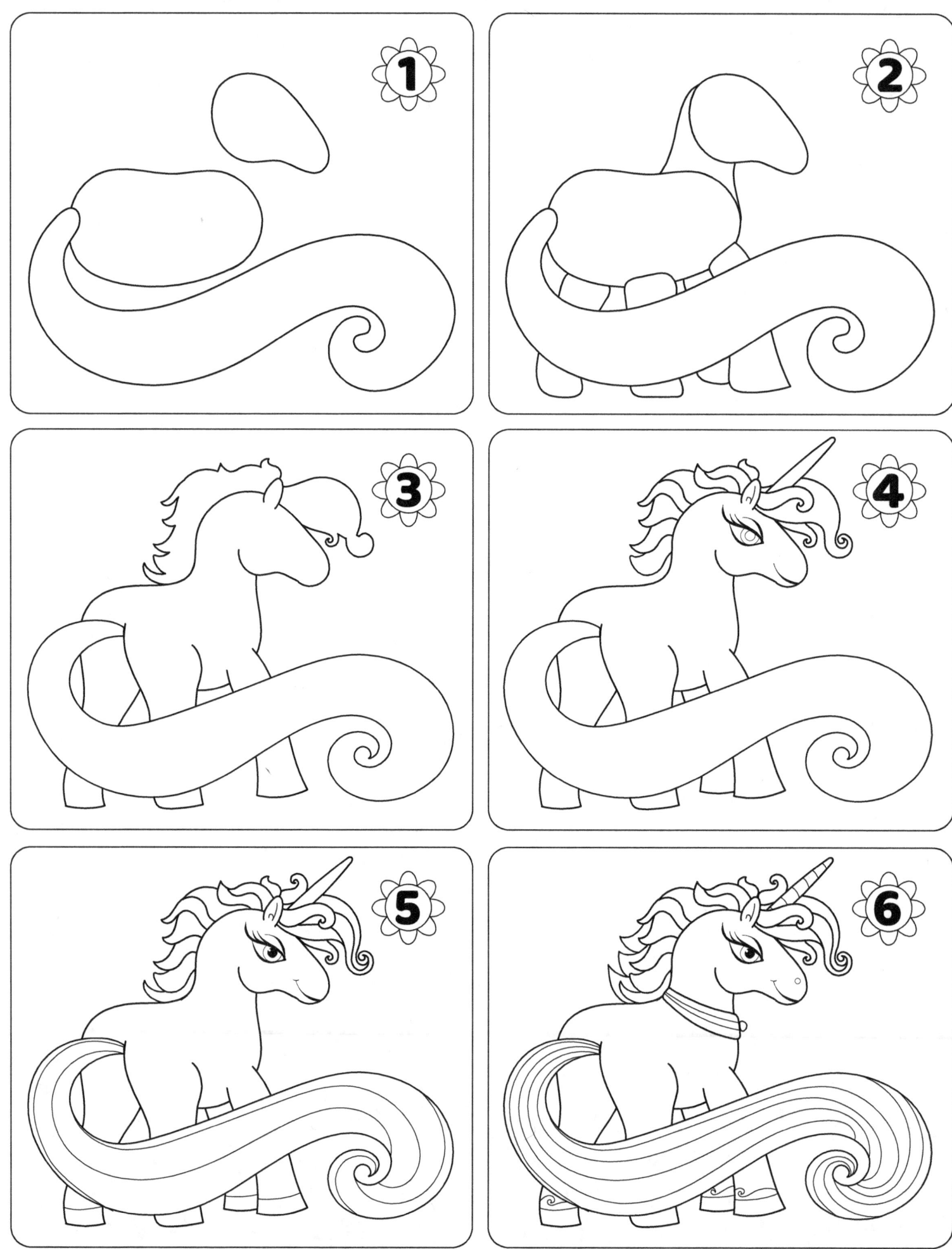

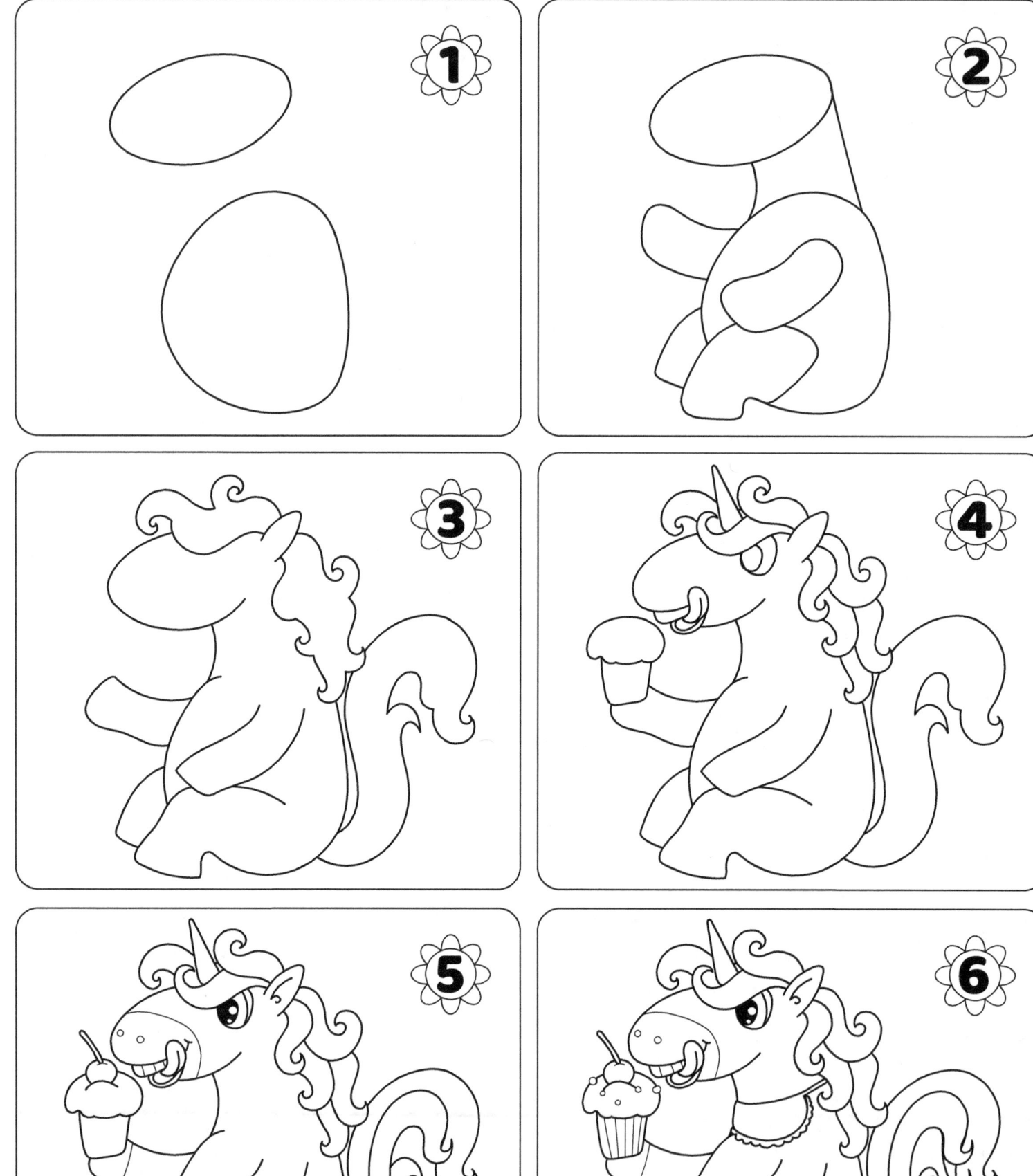

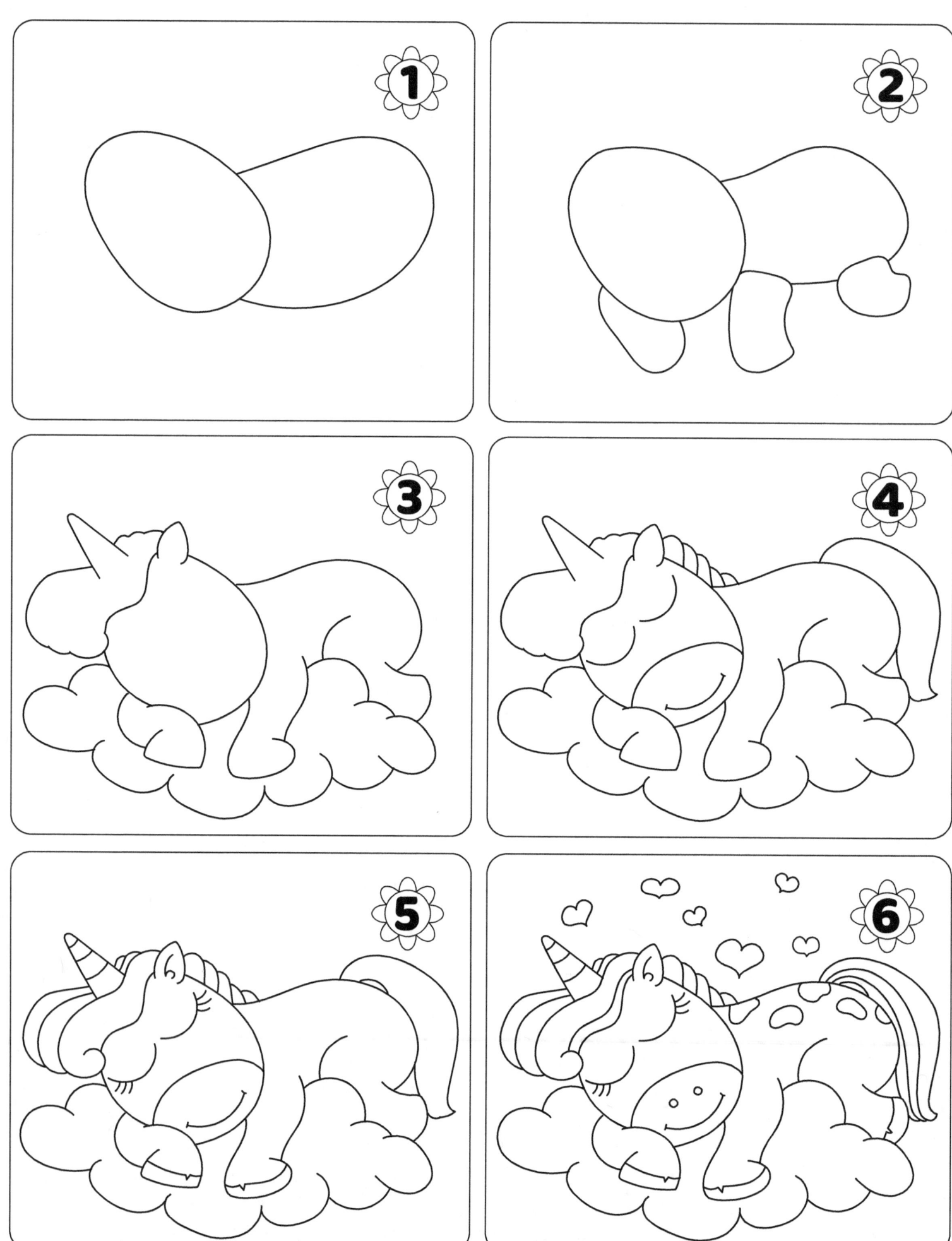

You Give It A Try!

You Give It A Try!

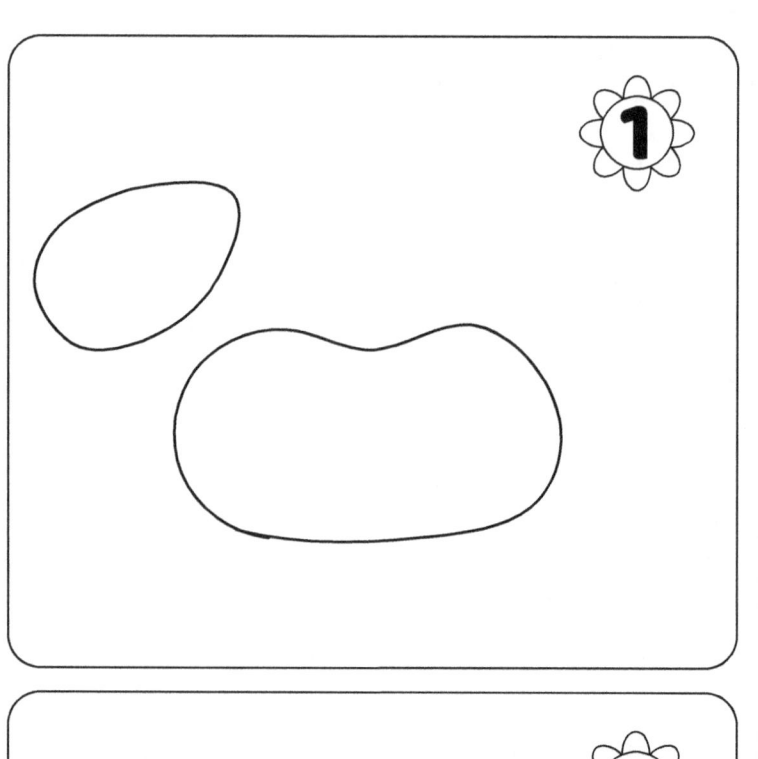
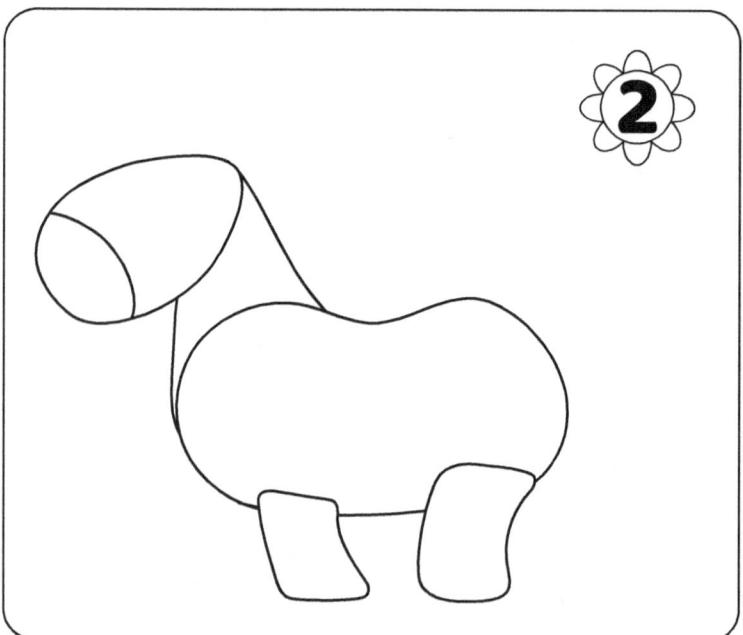
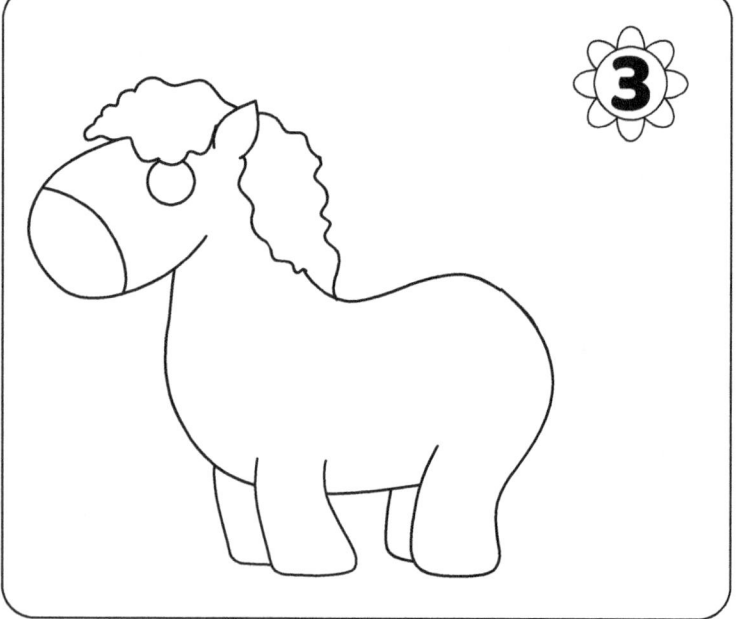
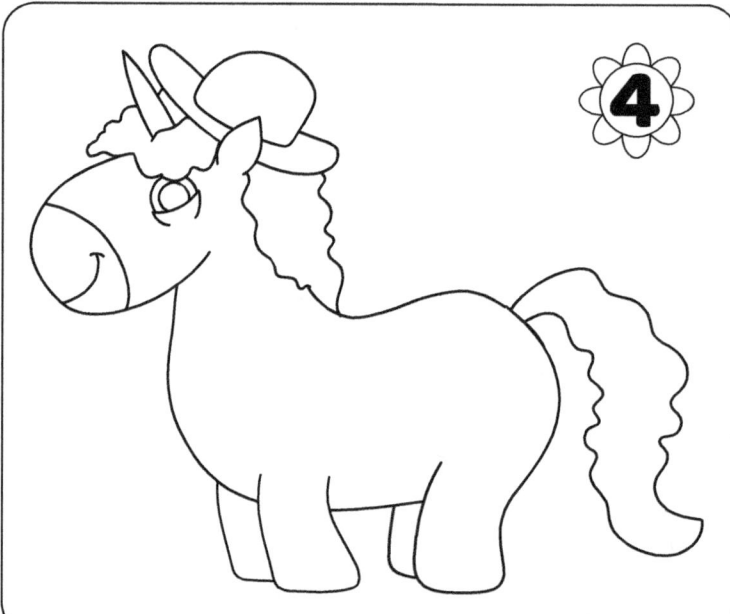
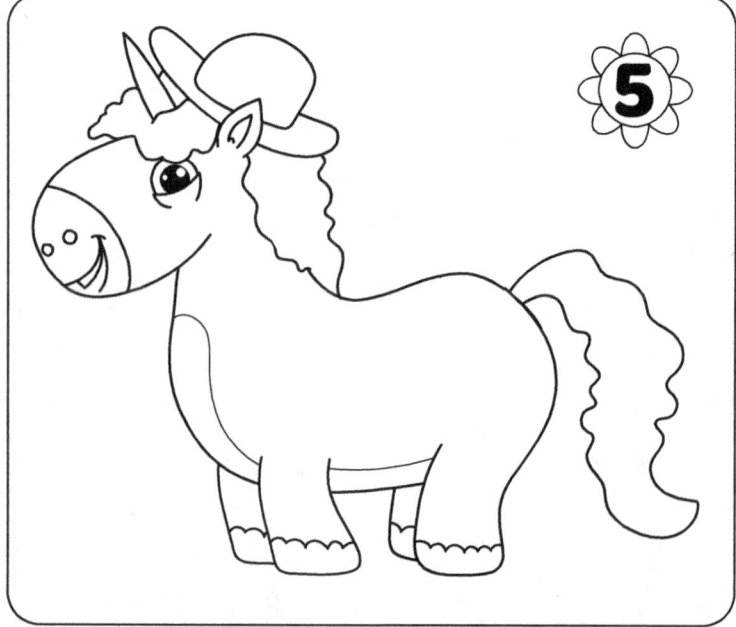
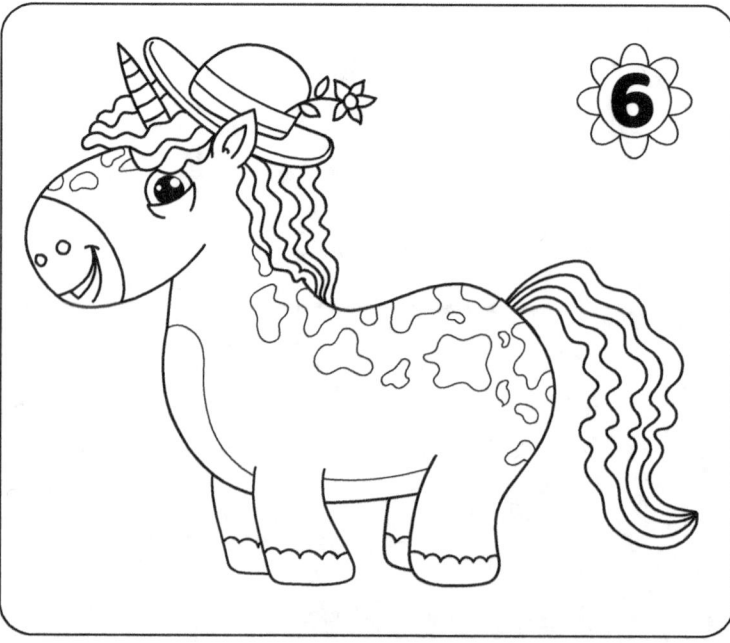

You Give It A Try!

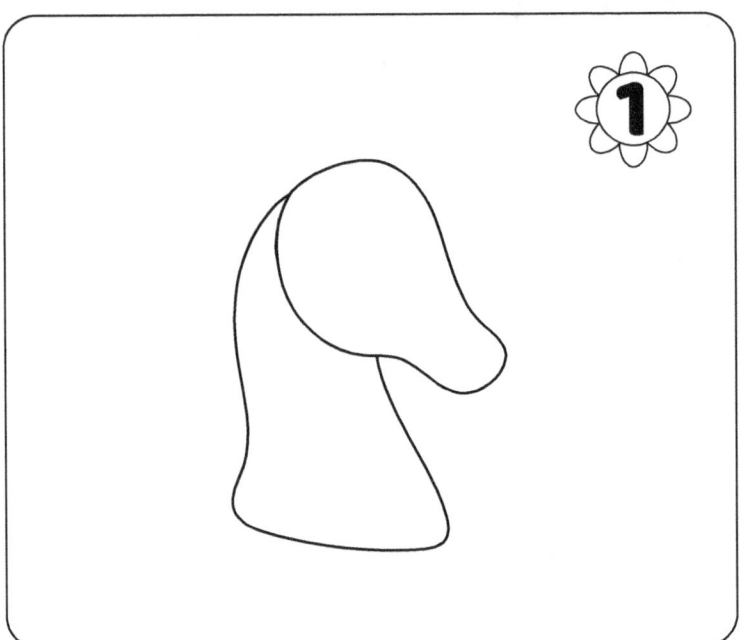
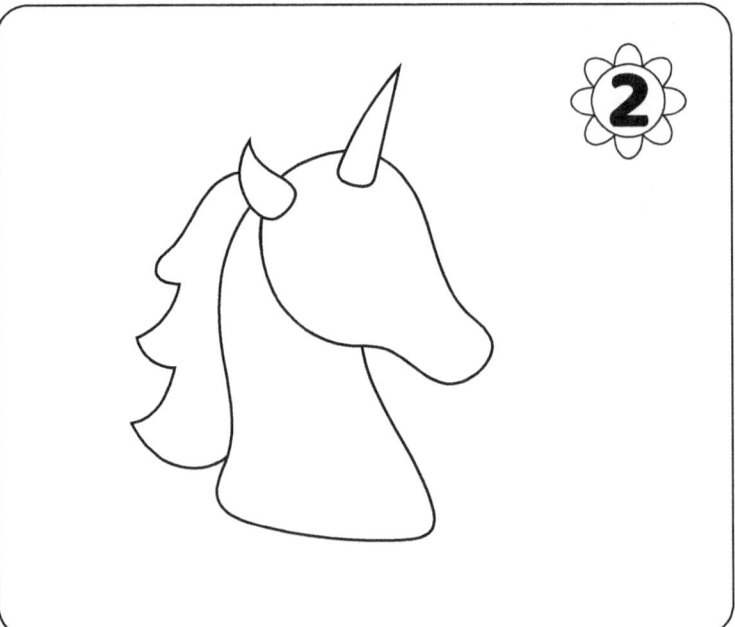
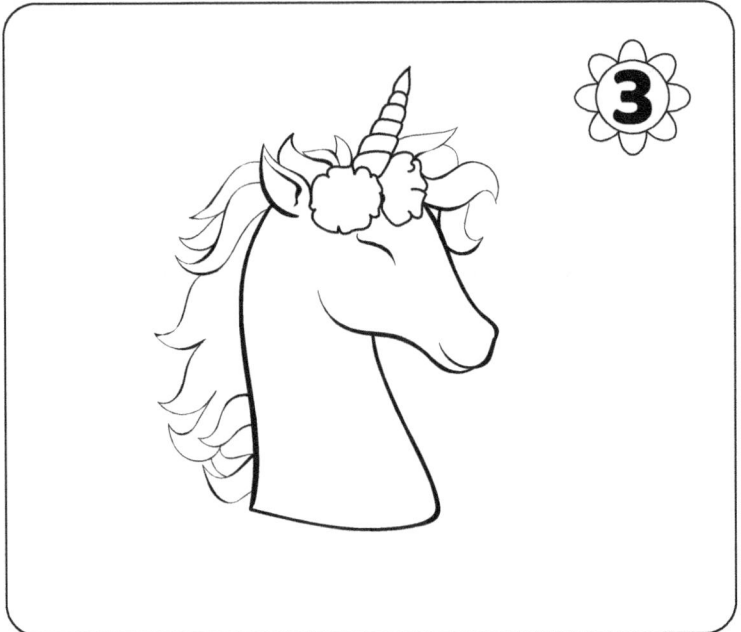
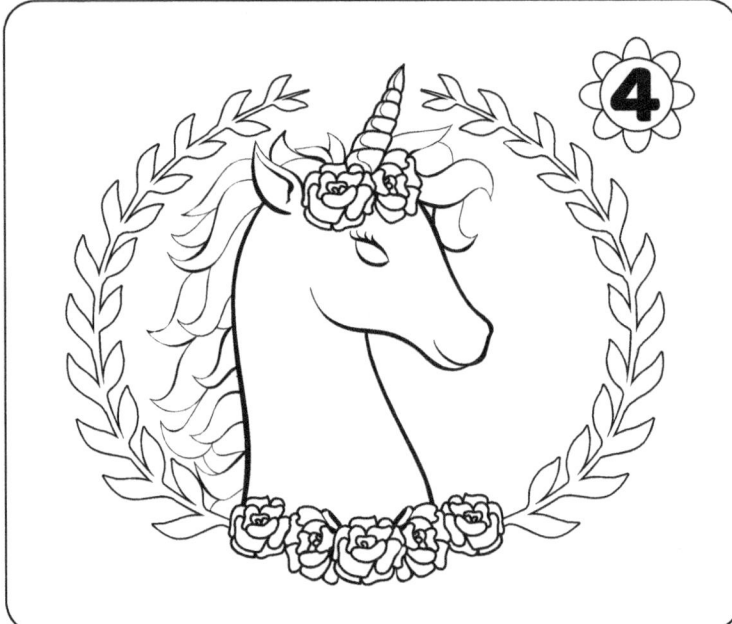
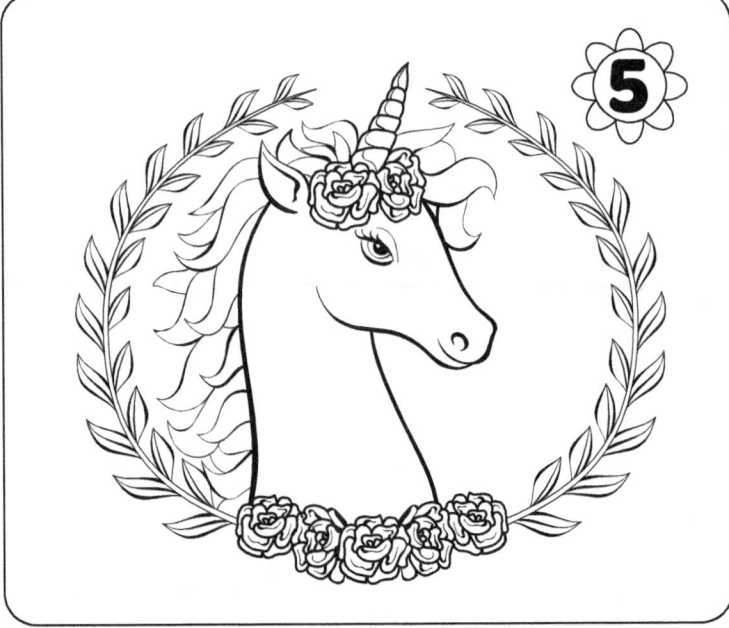
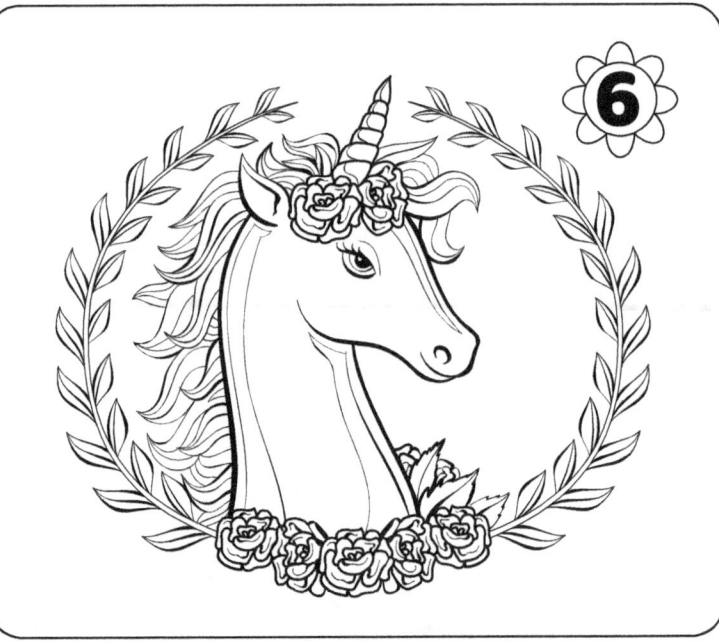

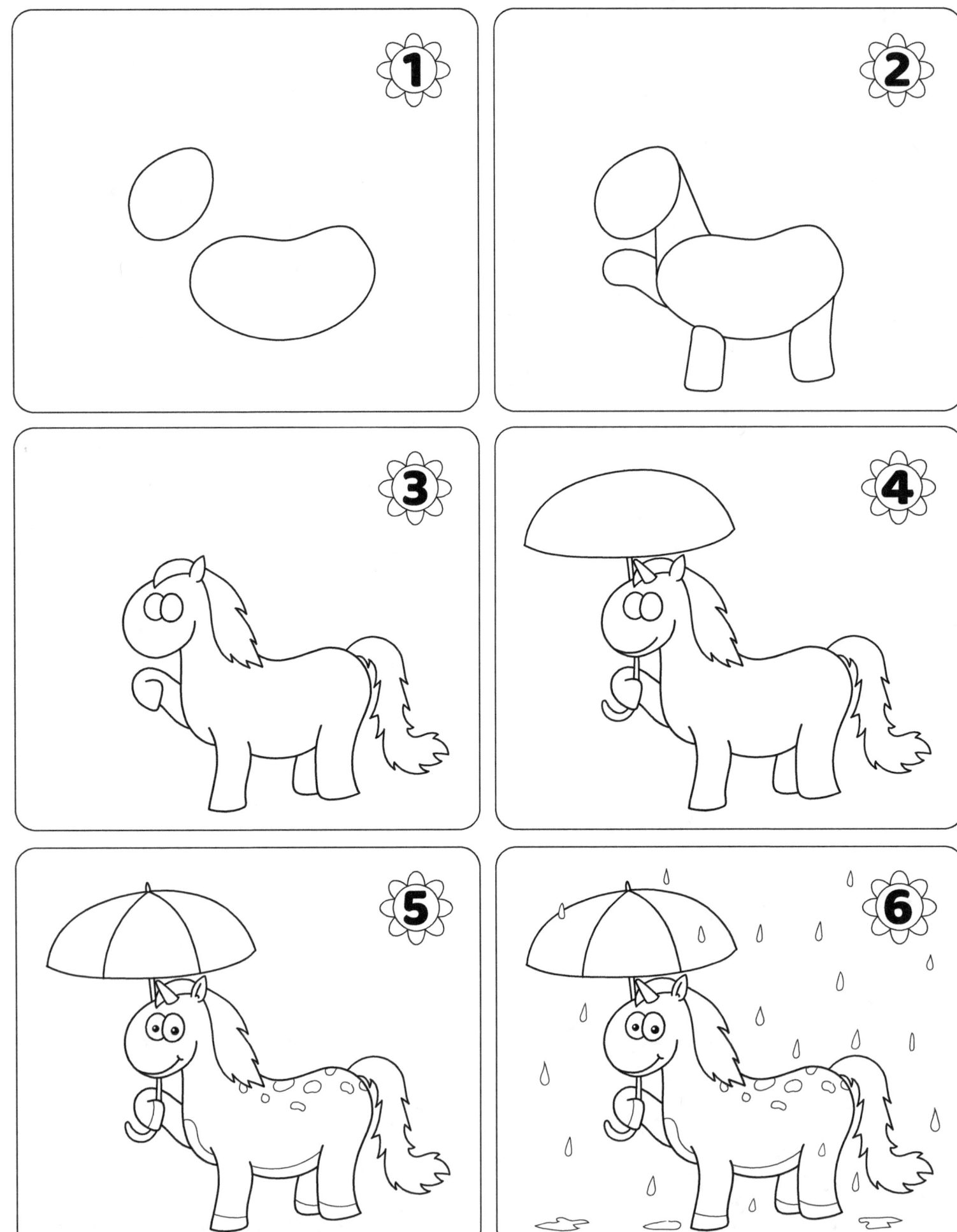

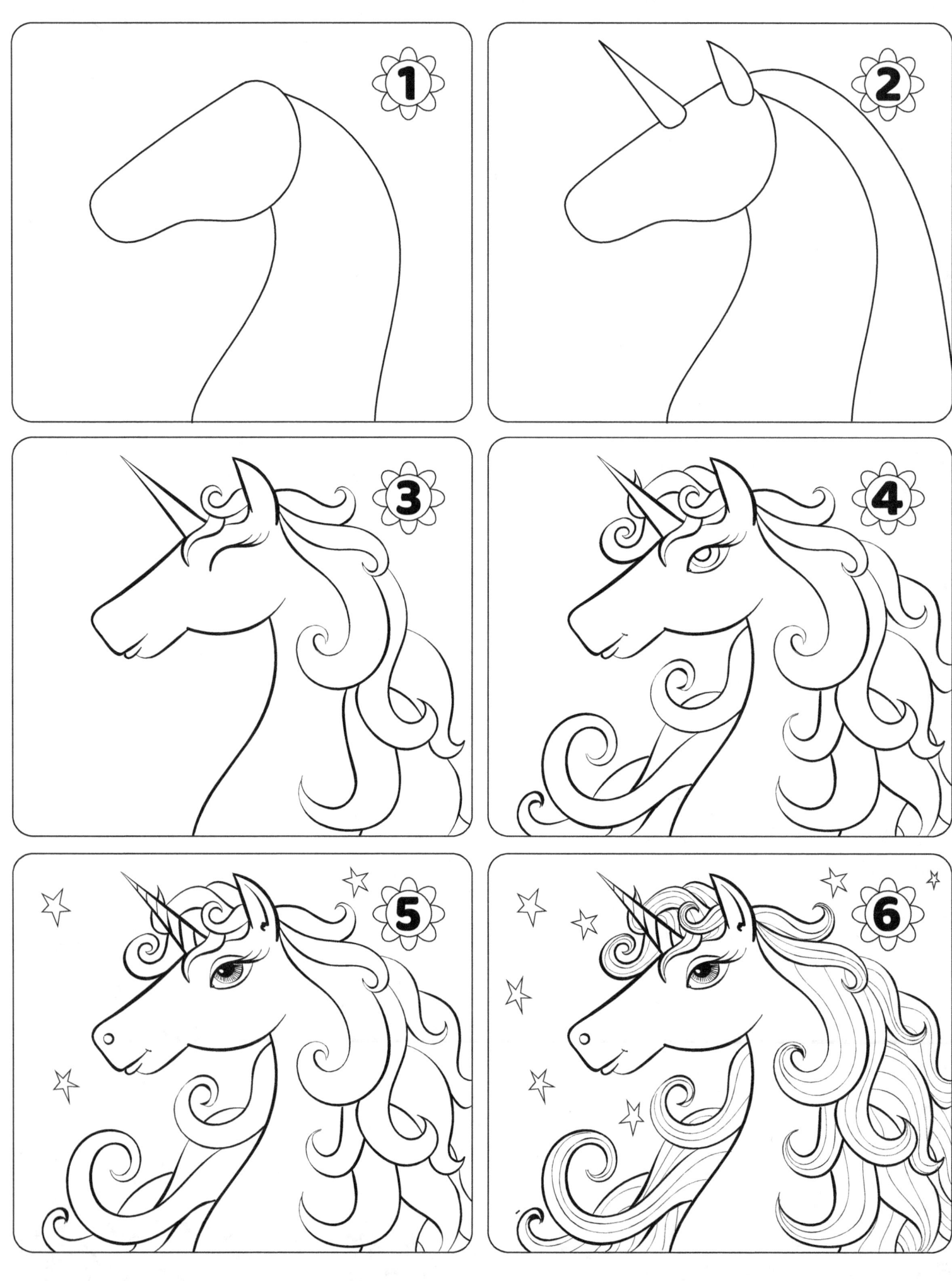

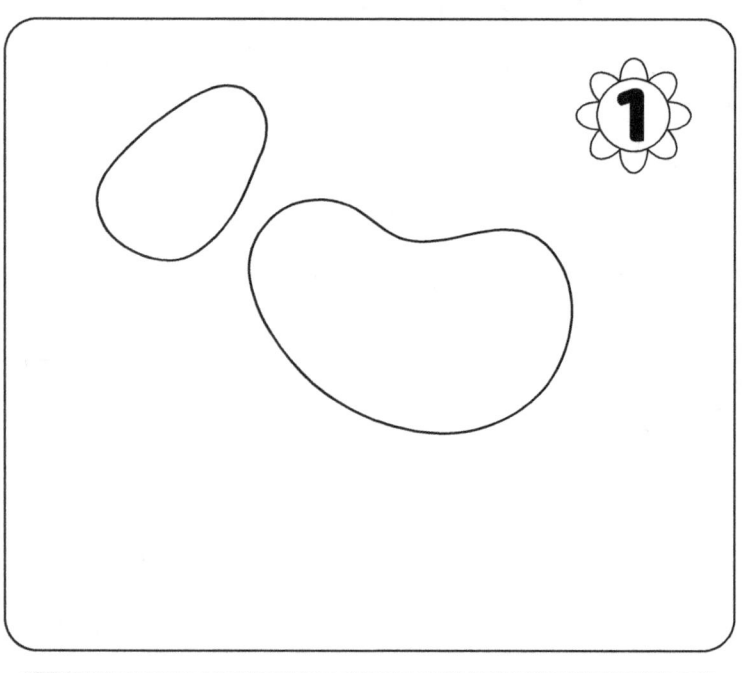

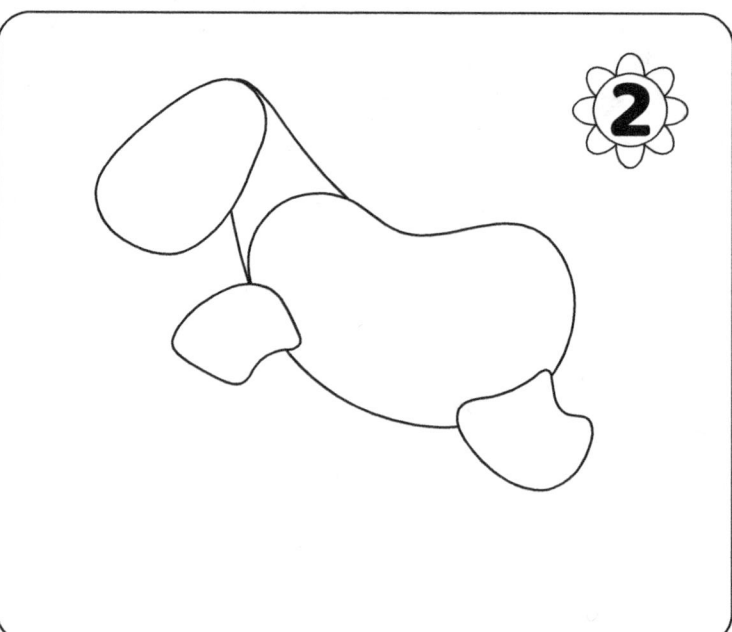

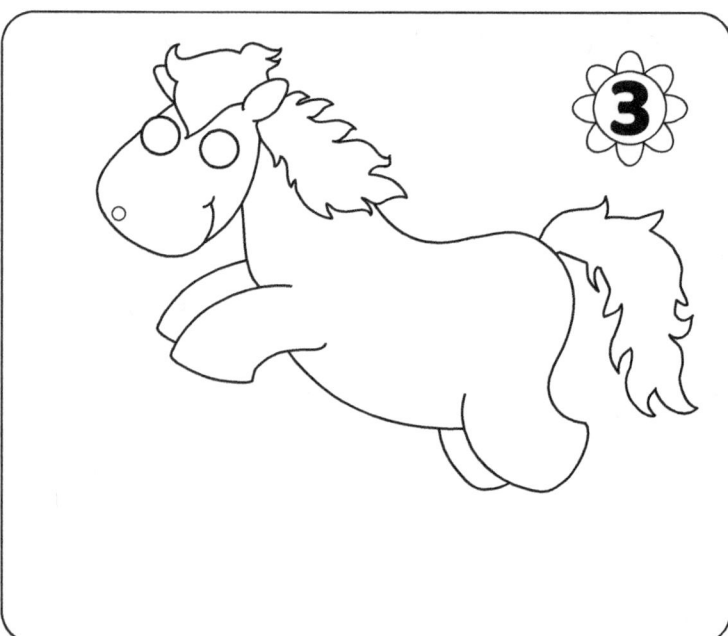

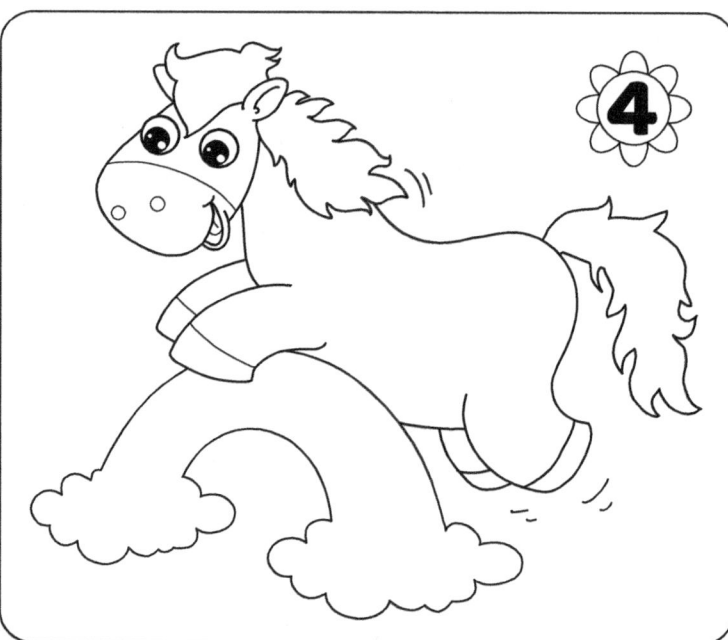

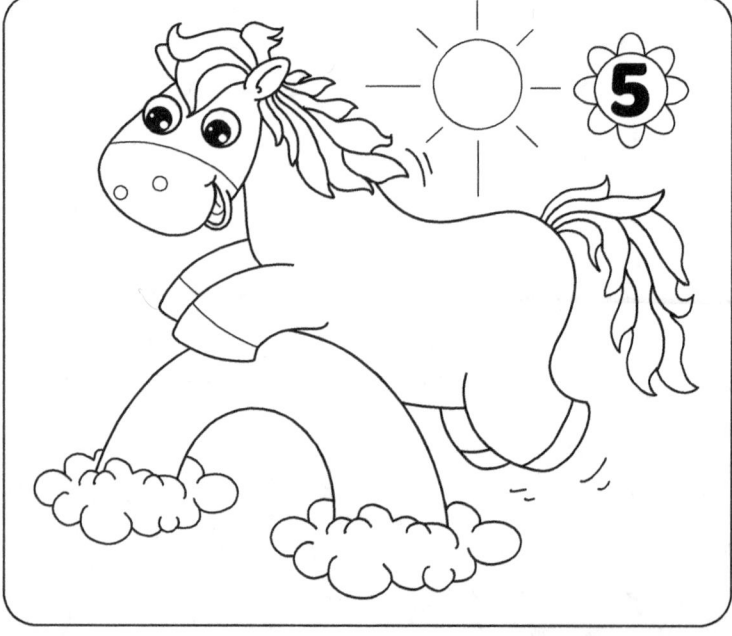

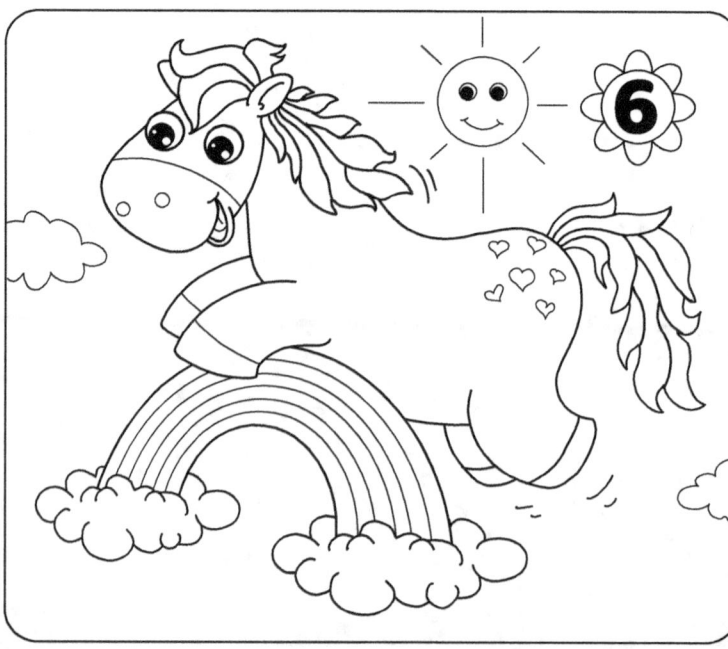

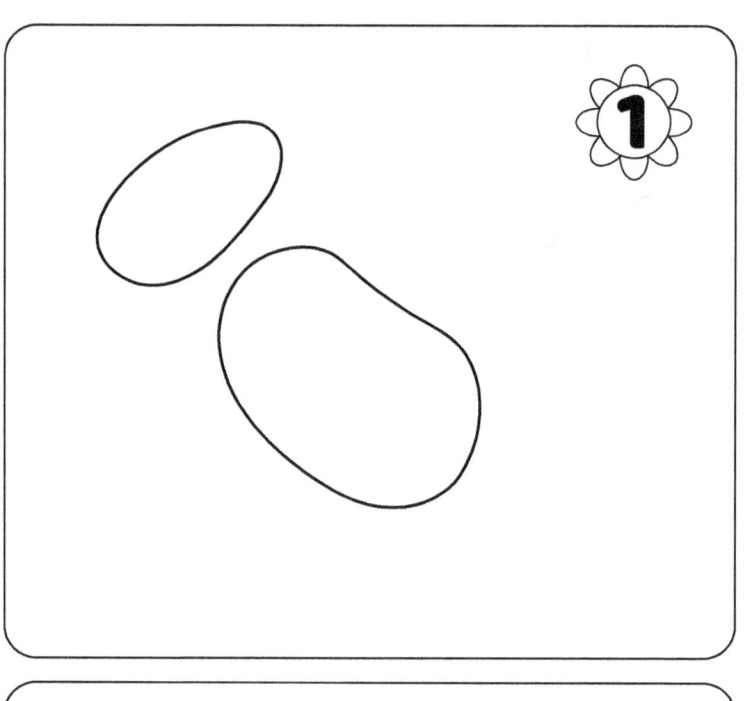

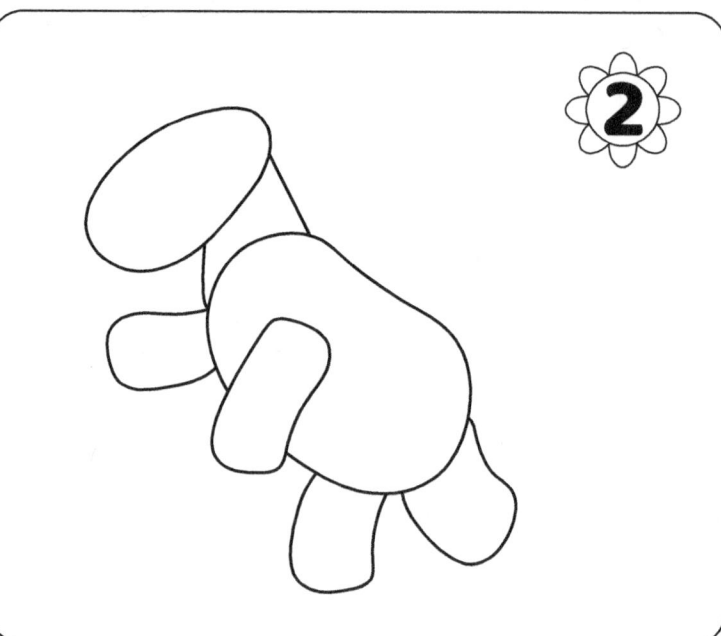

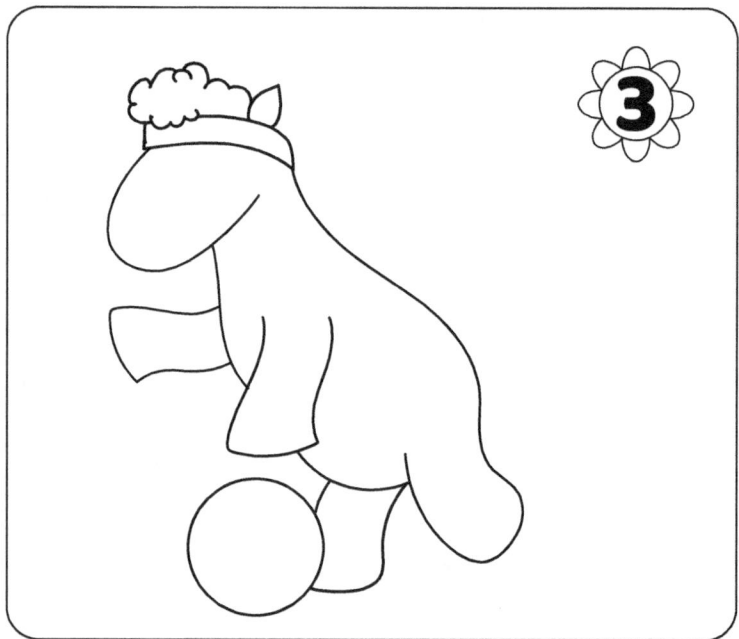

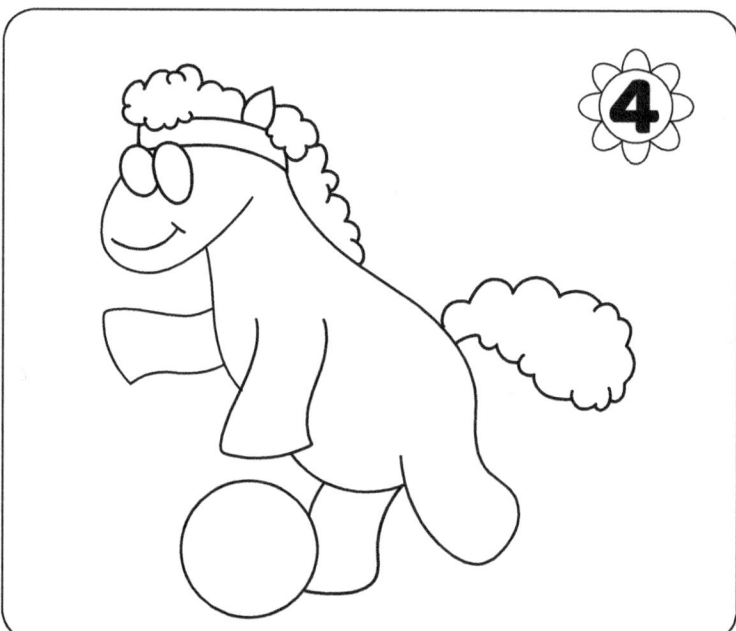

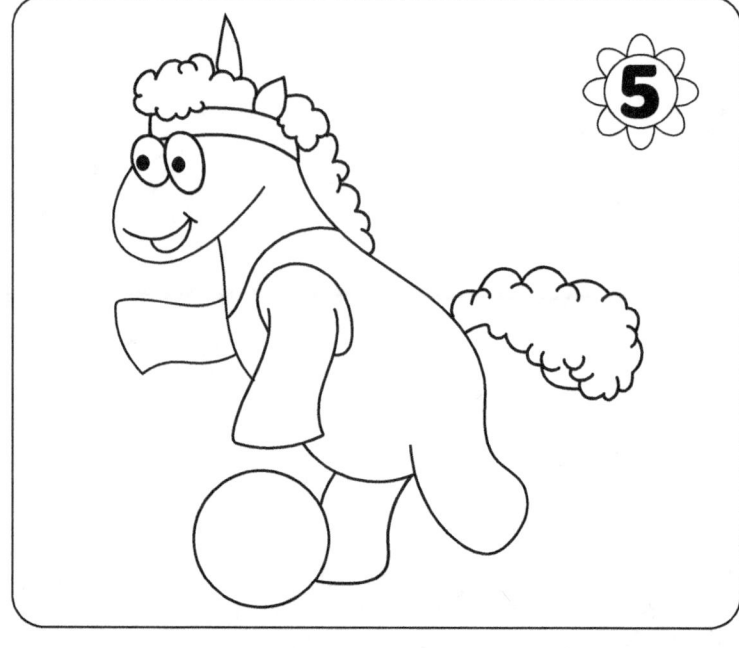

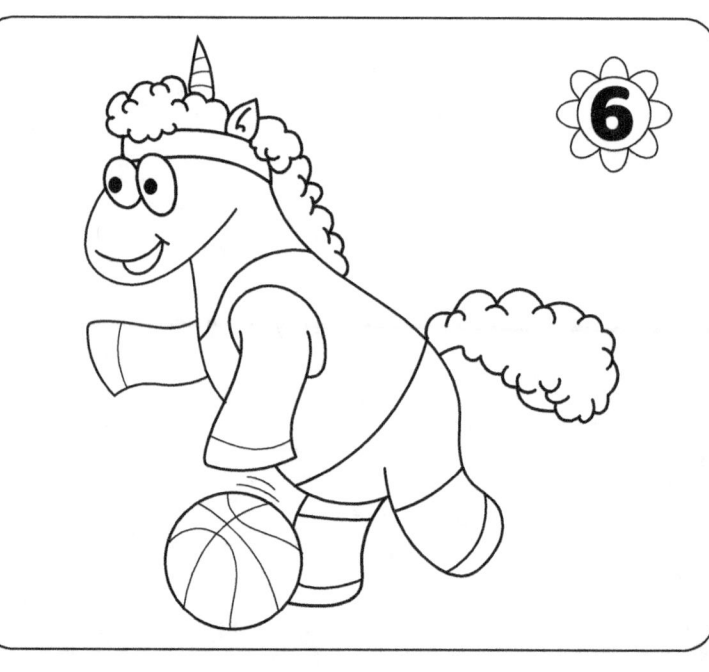

You Give It A Try!

You Give It A Try!

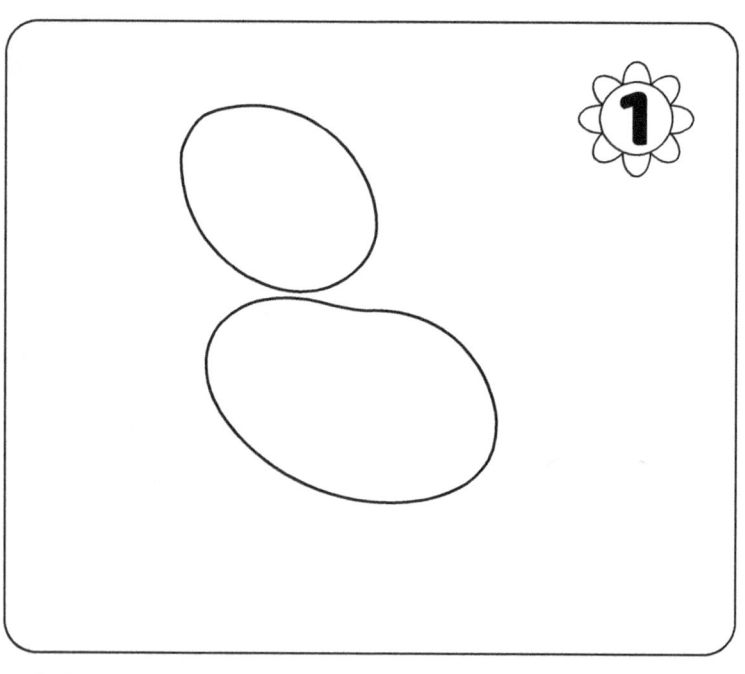

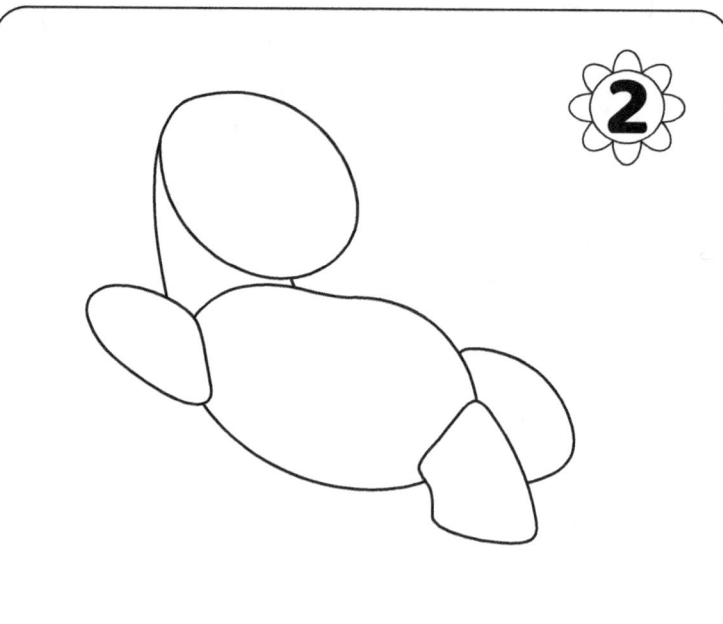

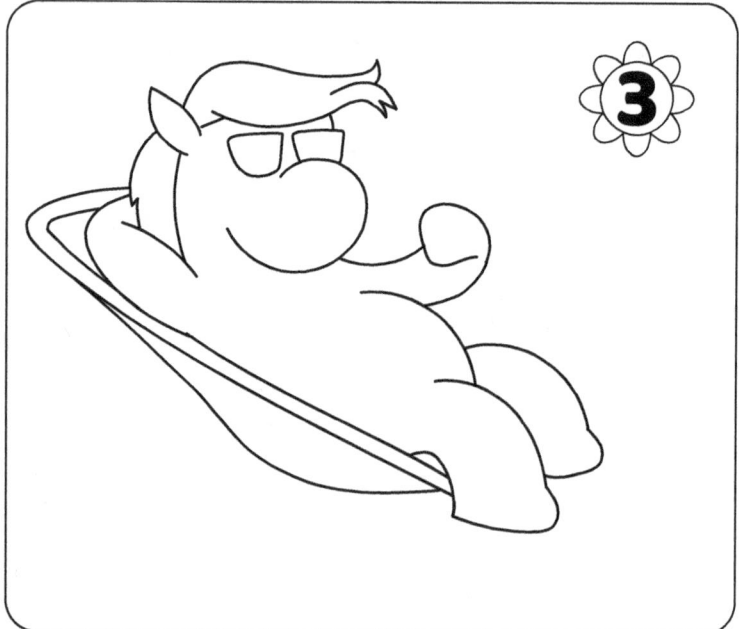

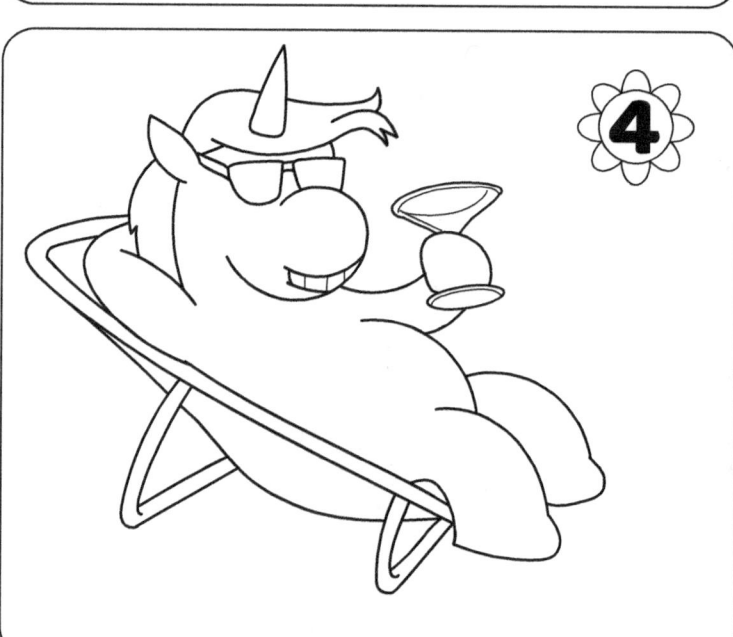

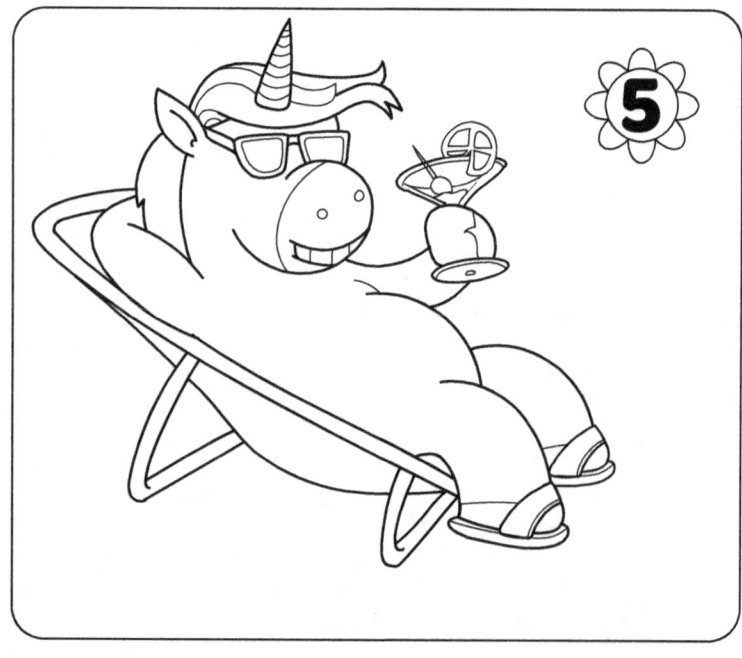

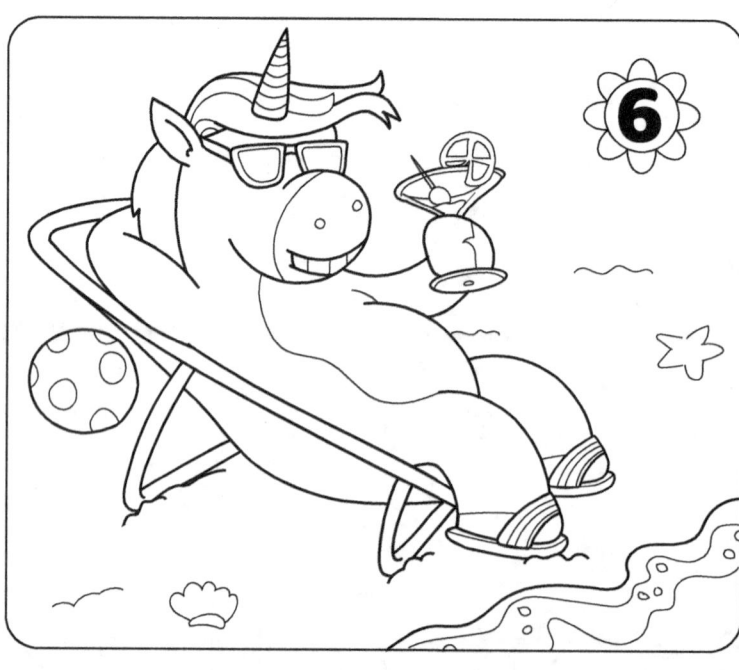

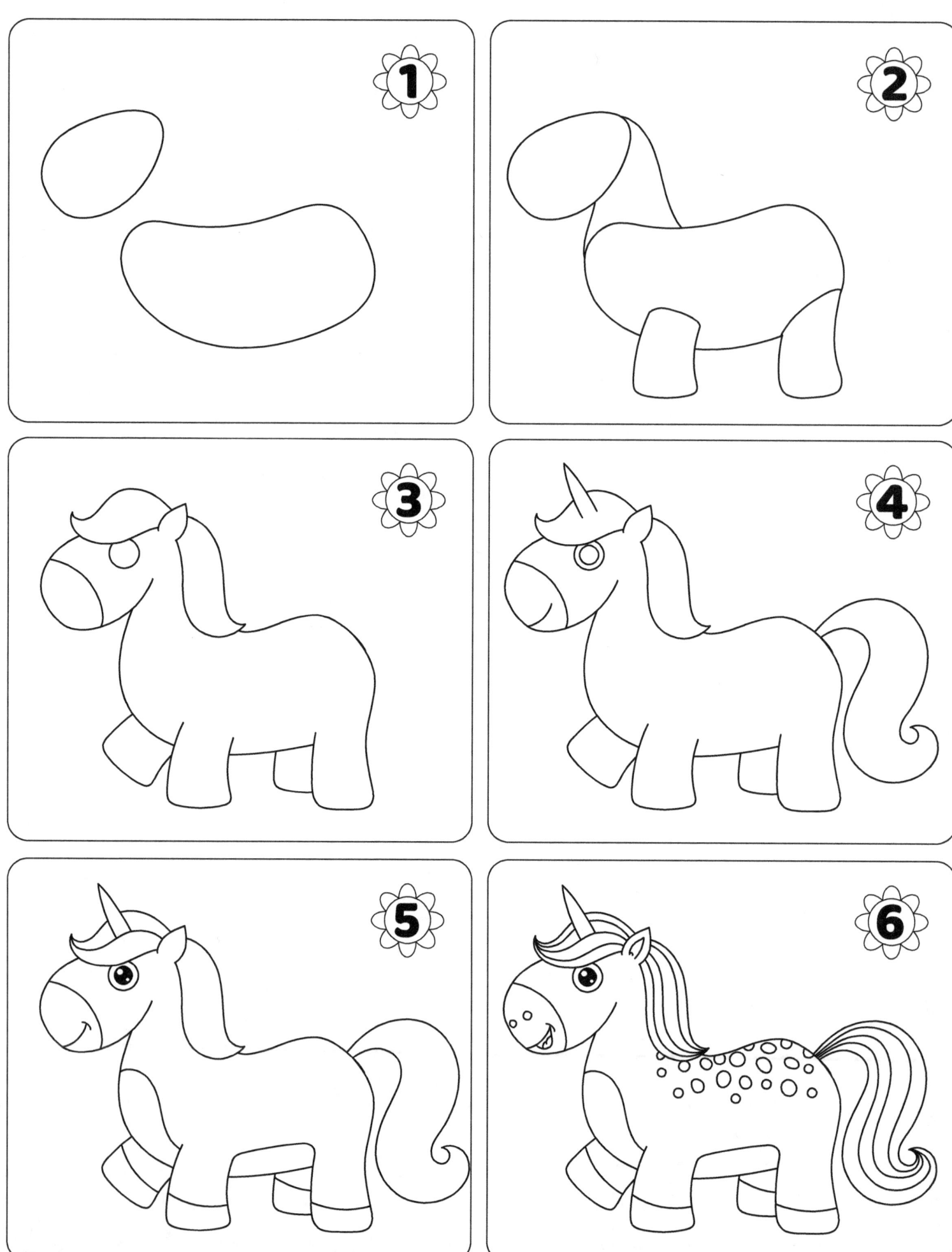

You Give It A Try!

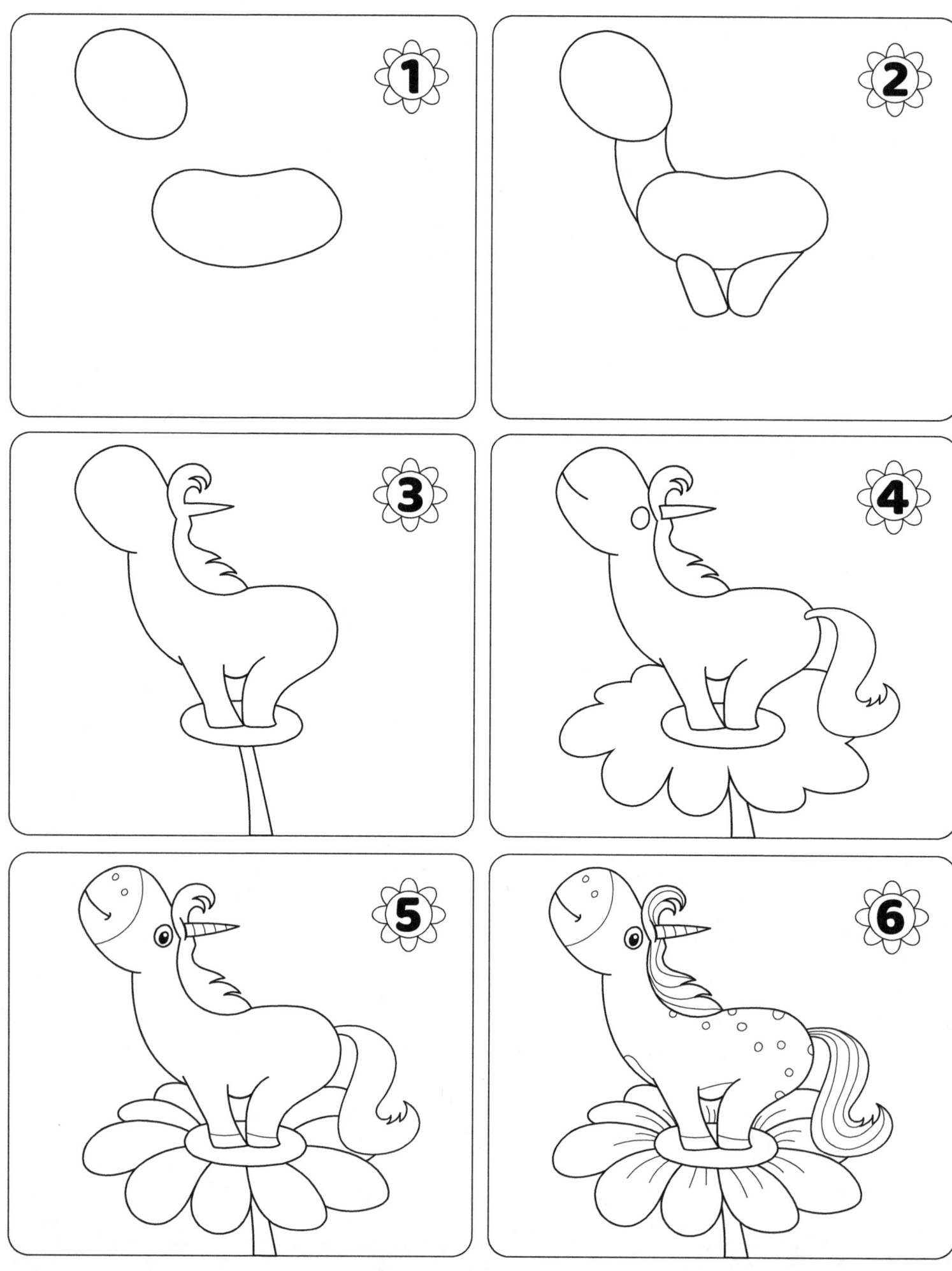

You Give It A Try!

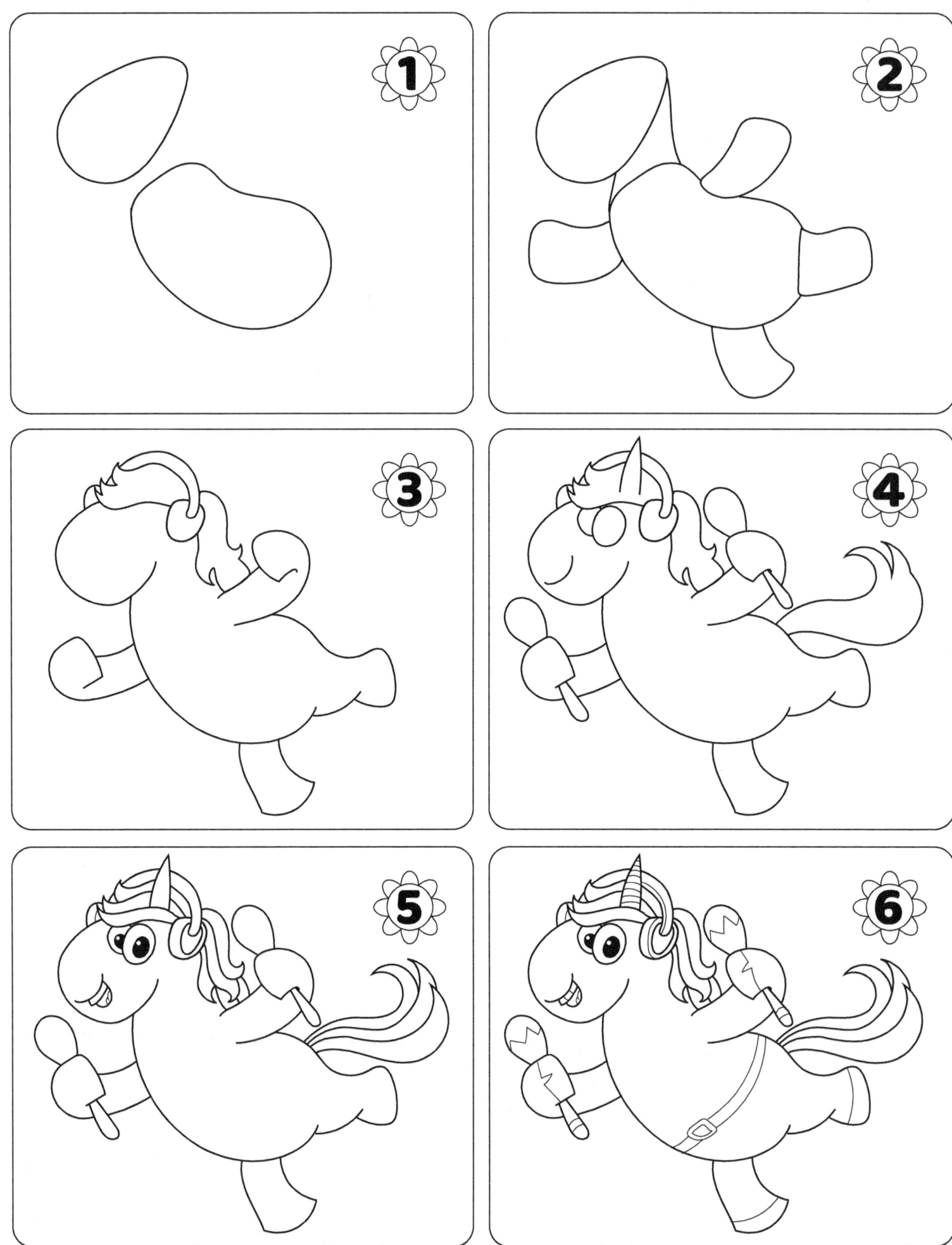

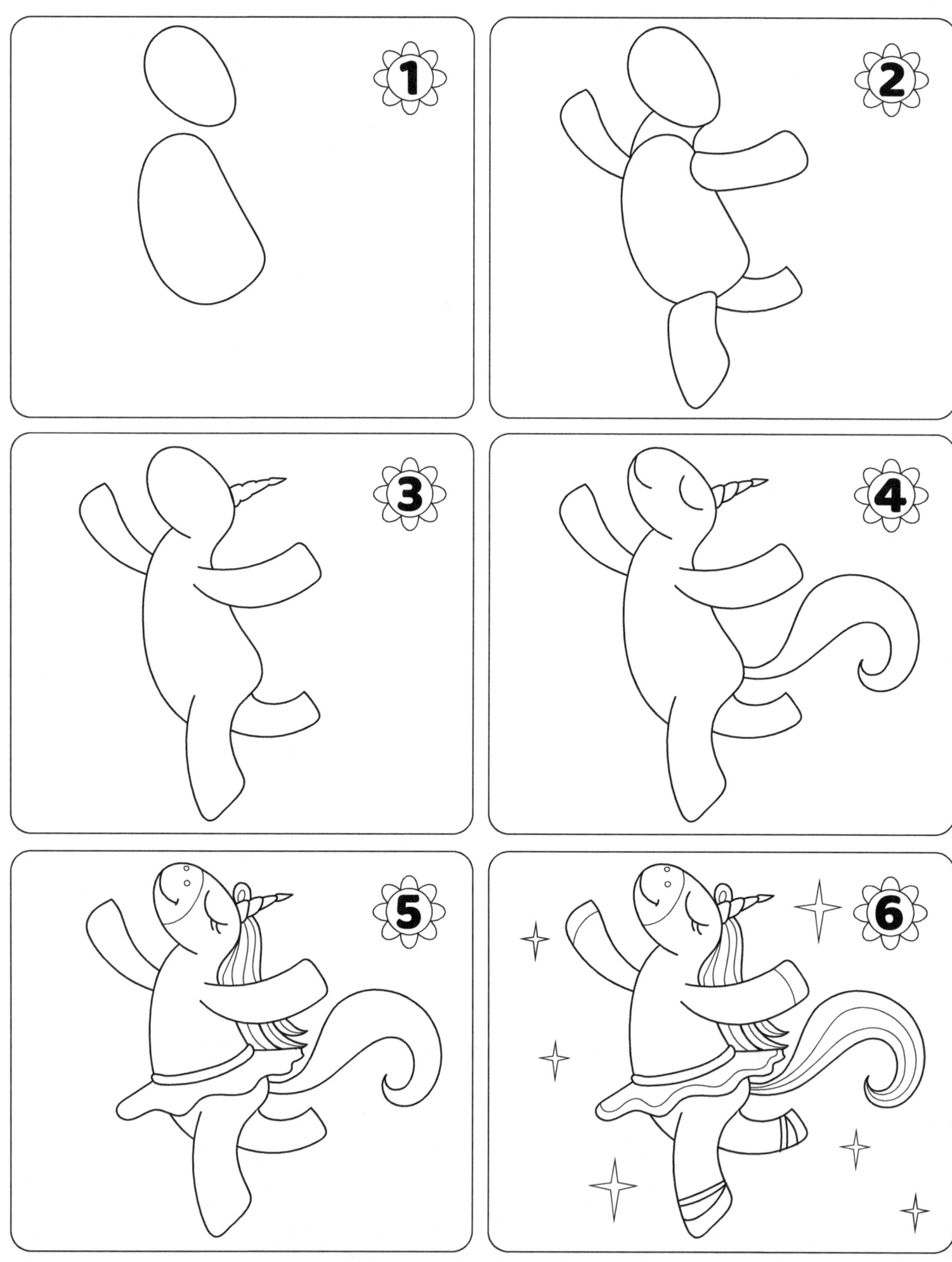

You Give It A Try!

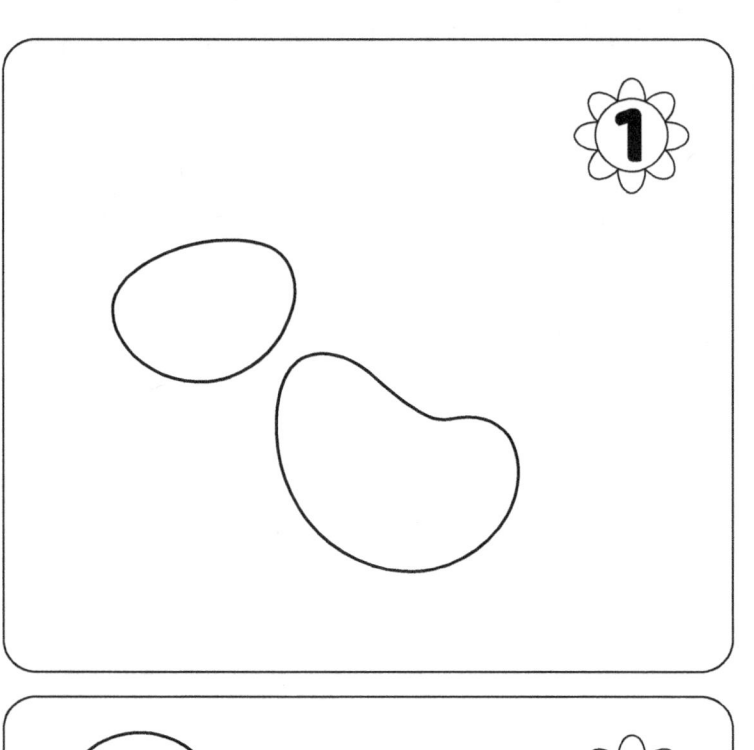

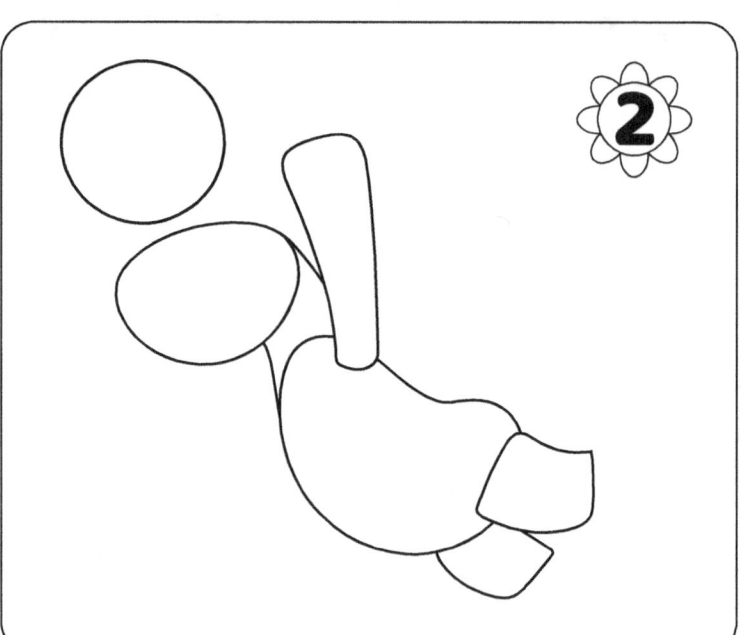

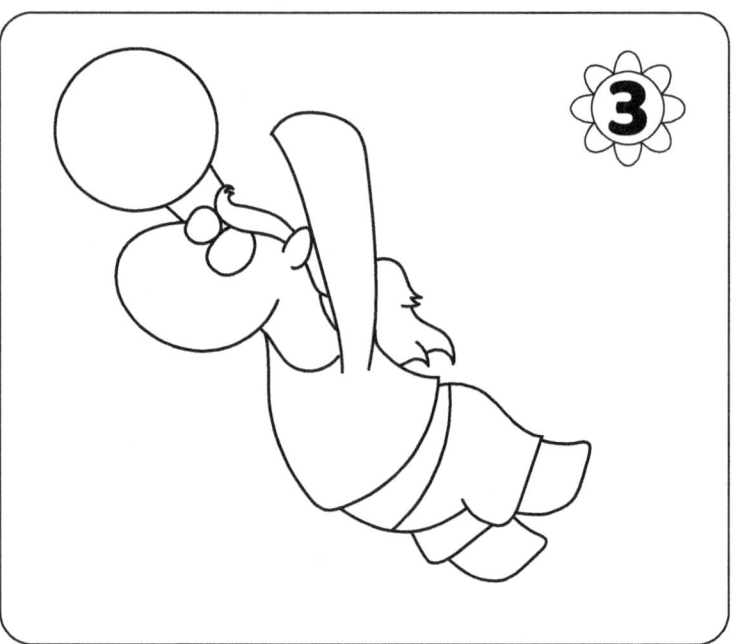

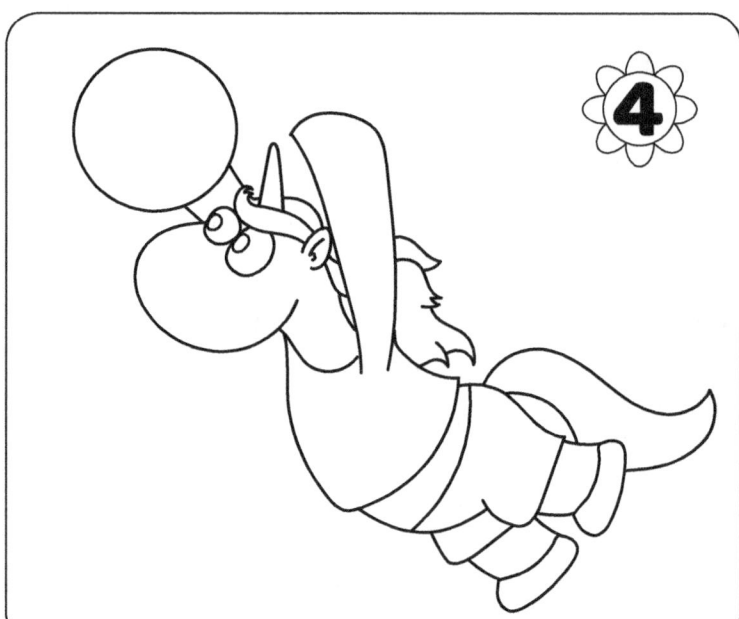

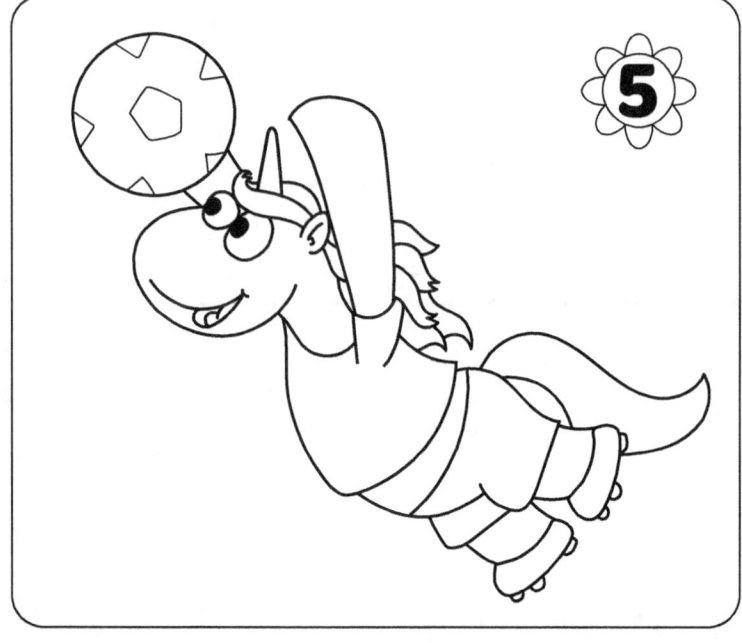

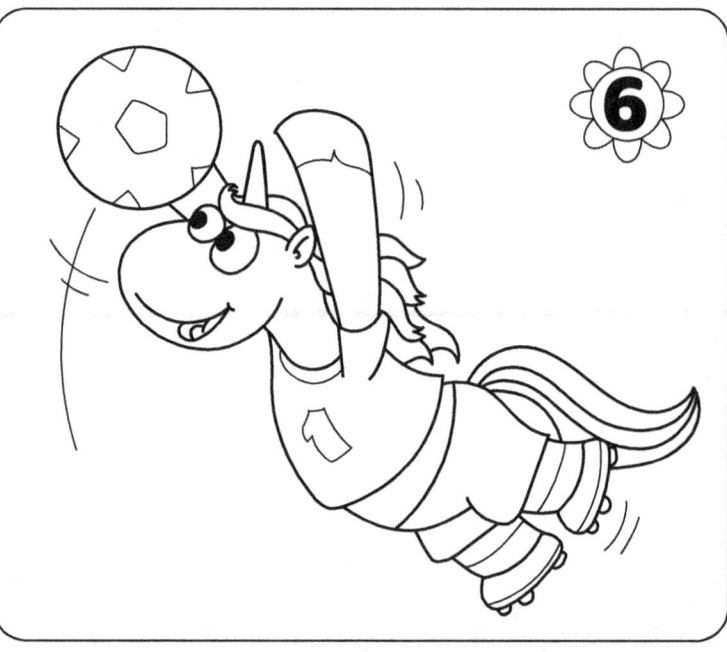

You Give It A Try!

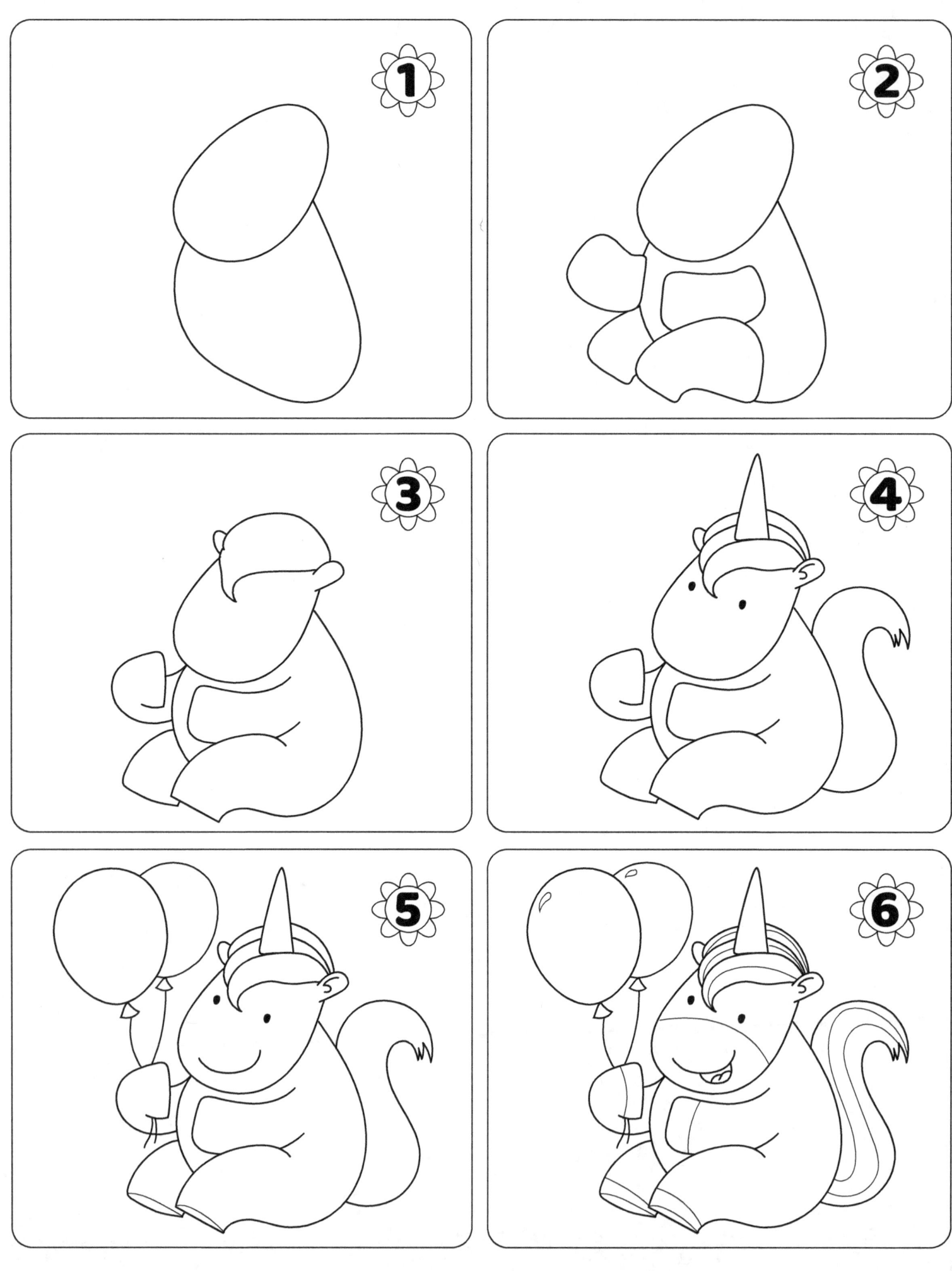

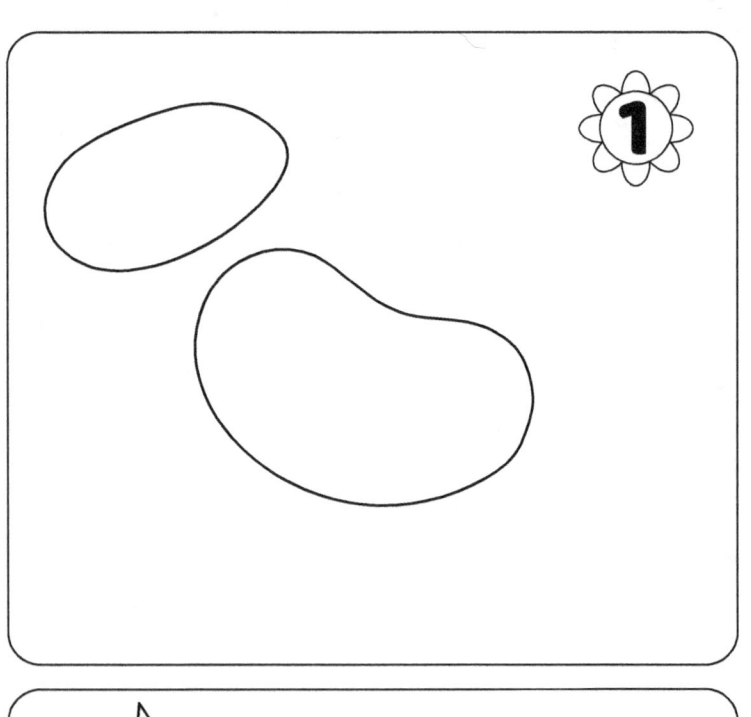

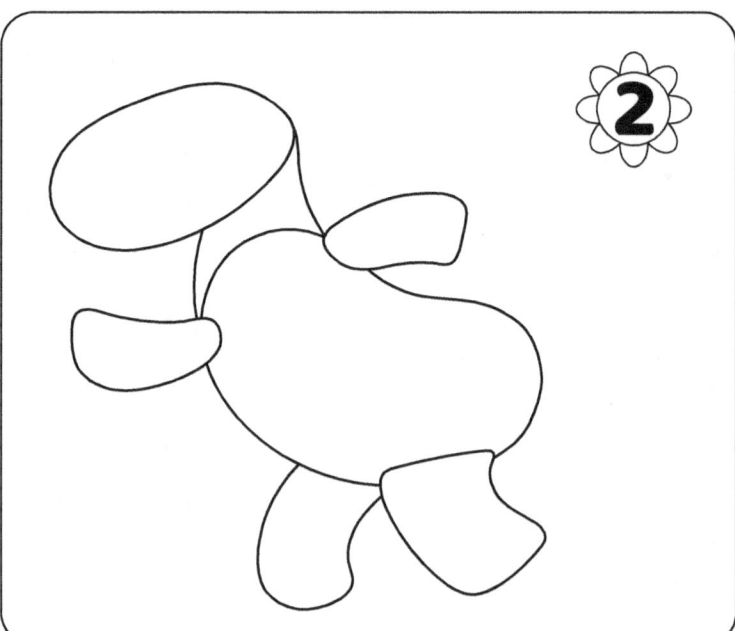

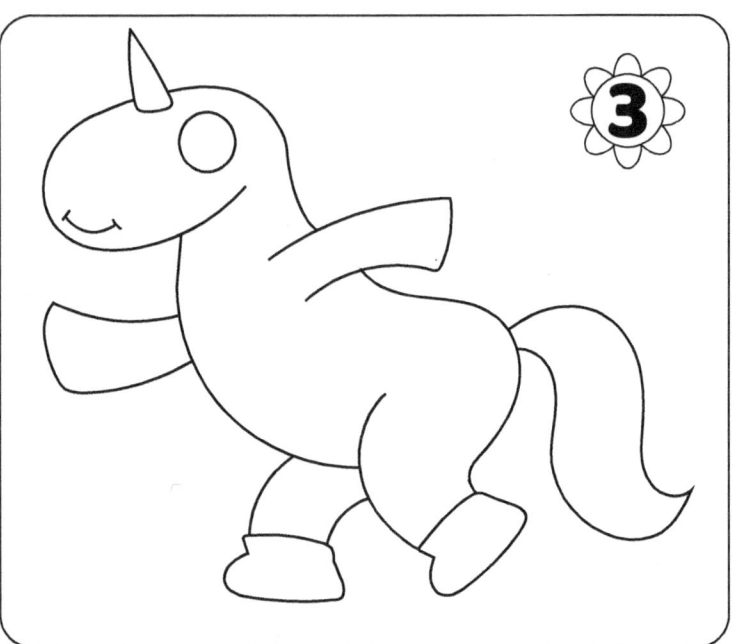

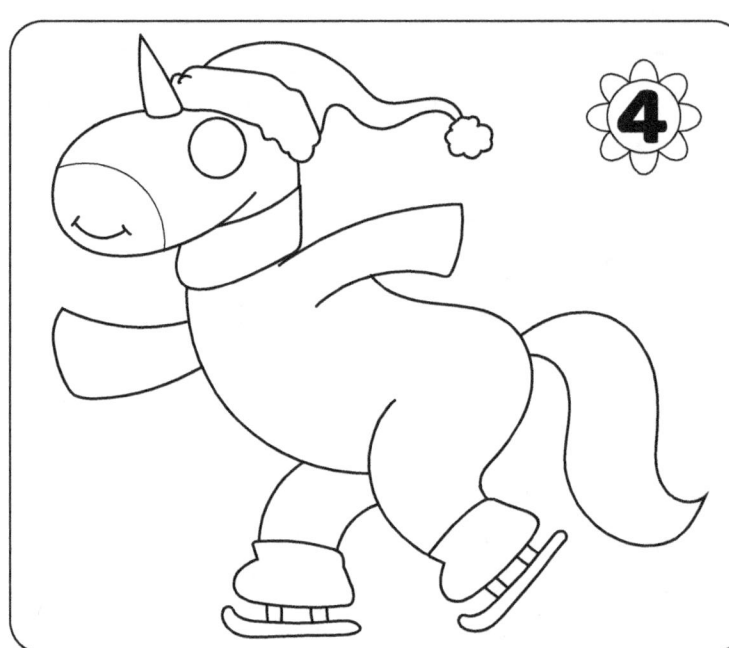

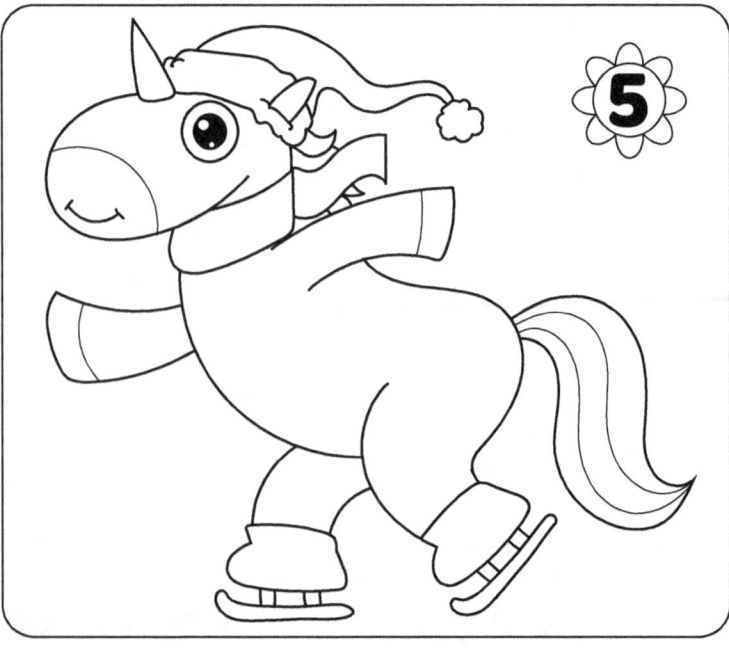

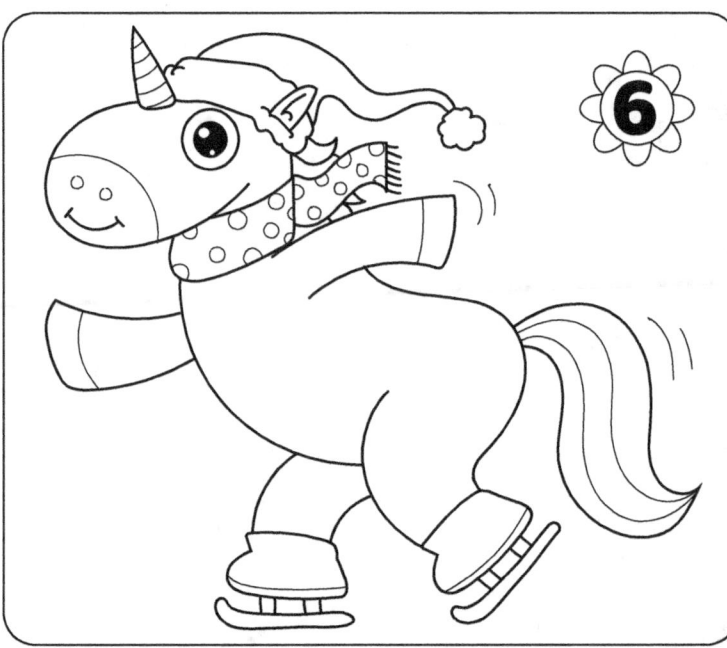

You Give It A Try!

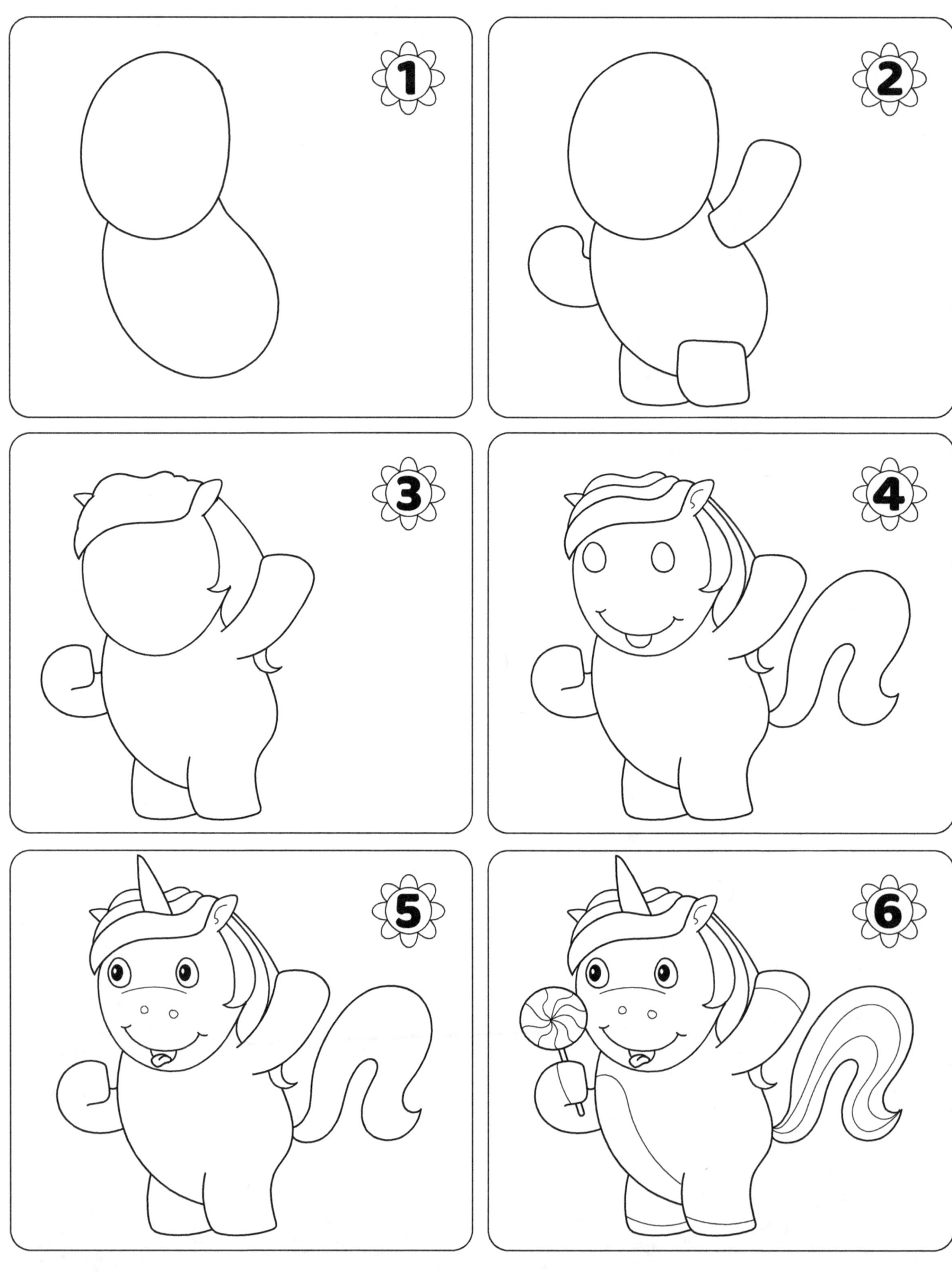

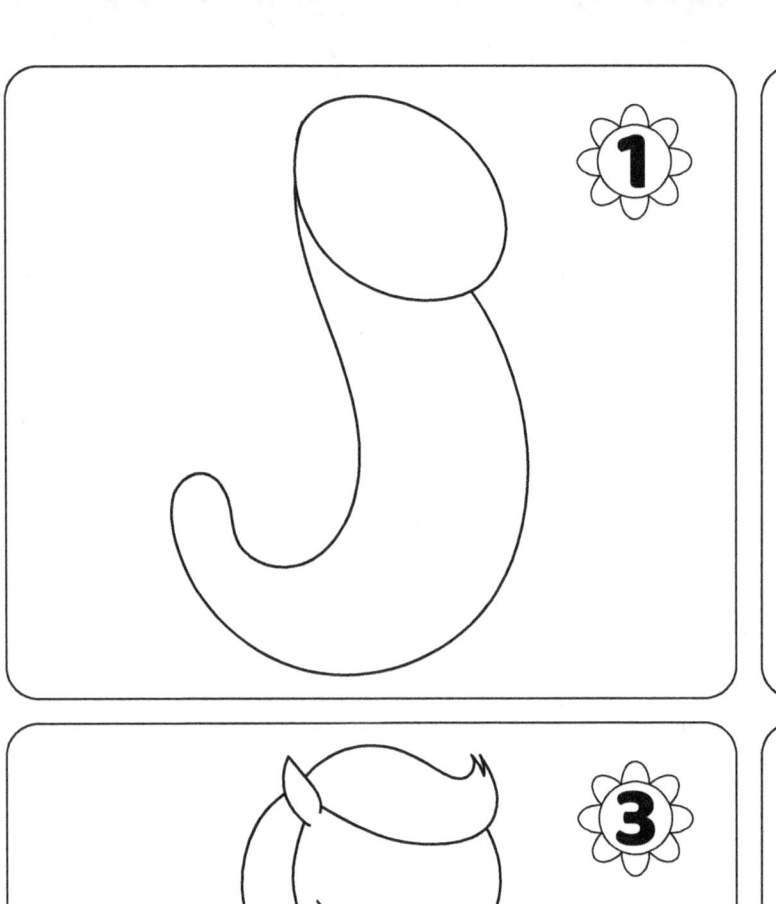

1

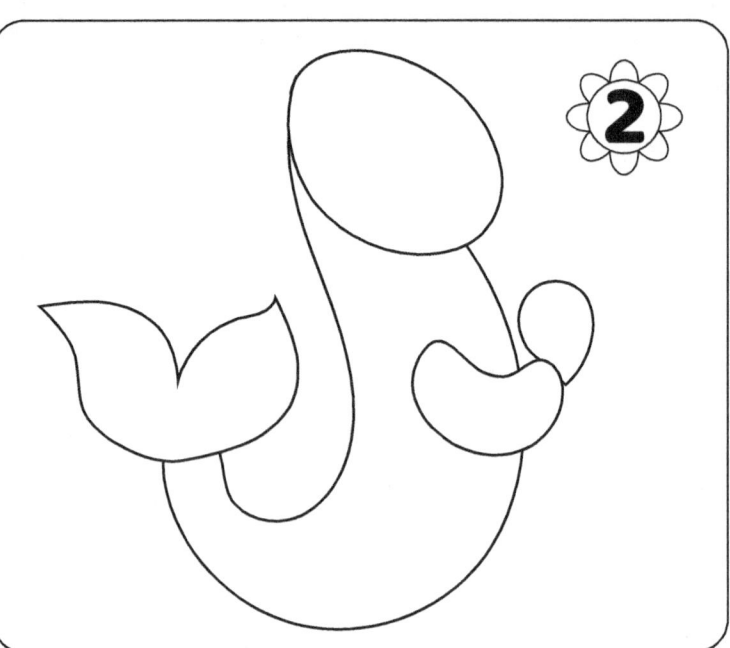

2

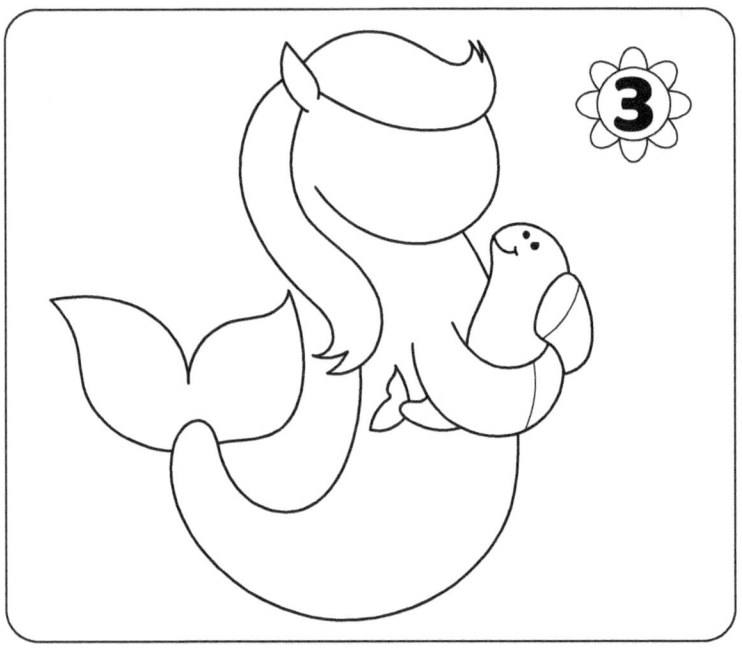

3

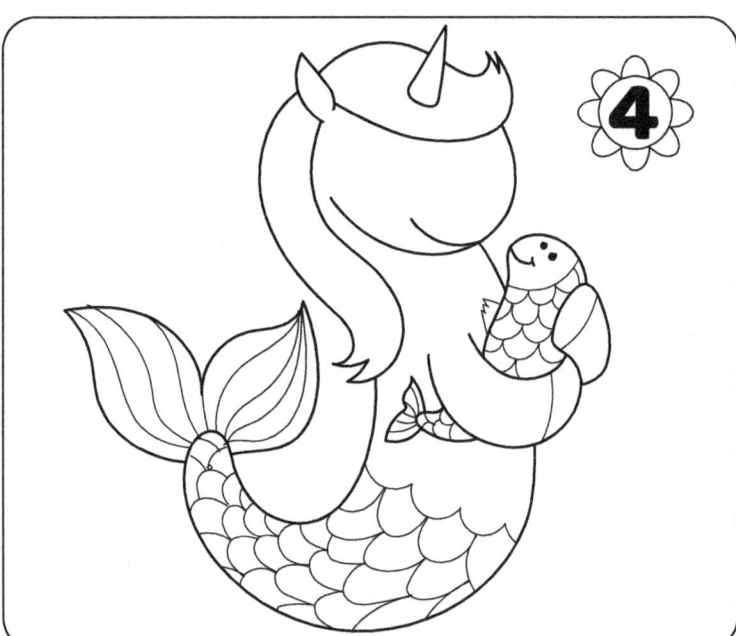

4

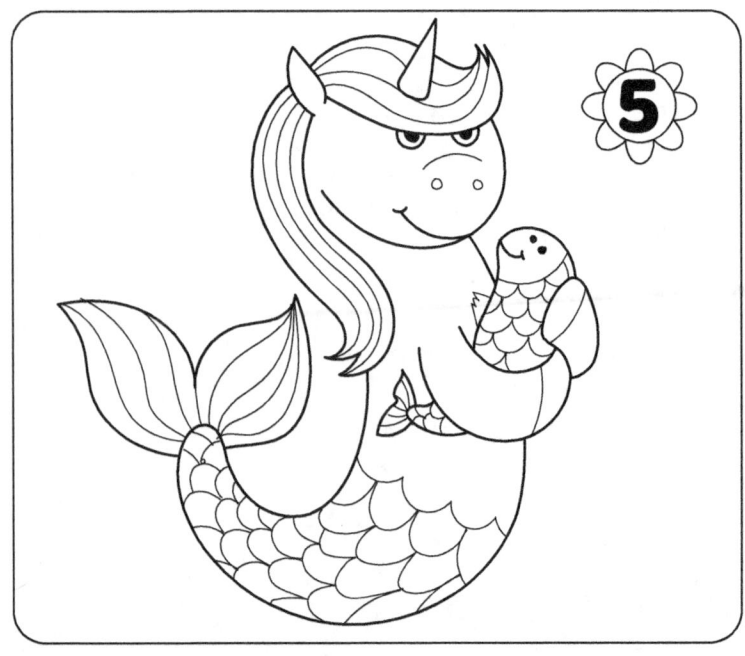

5

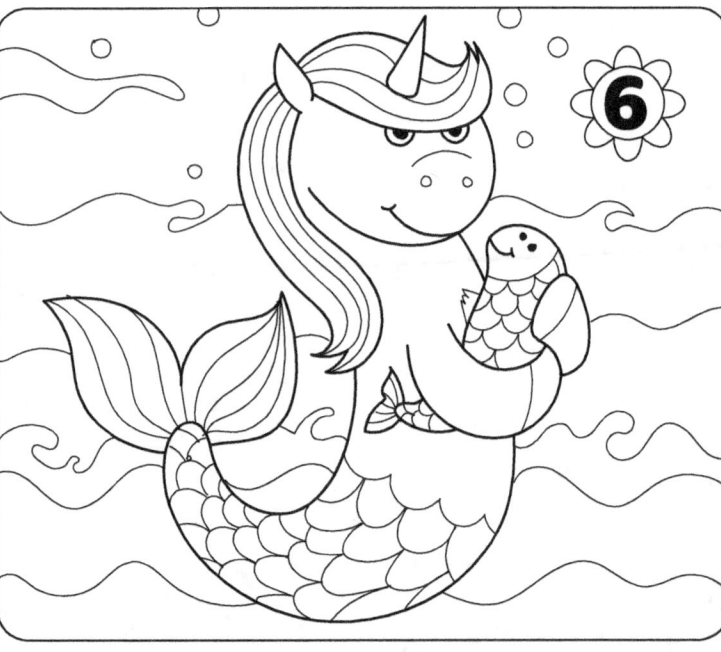

6

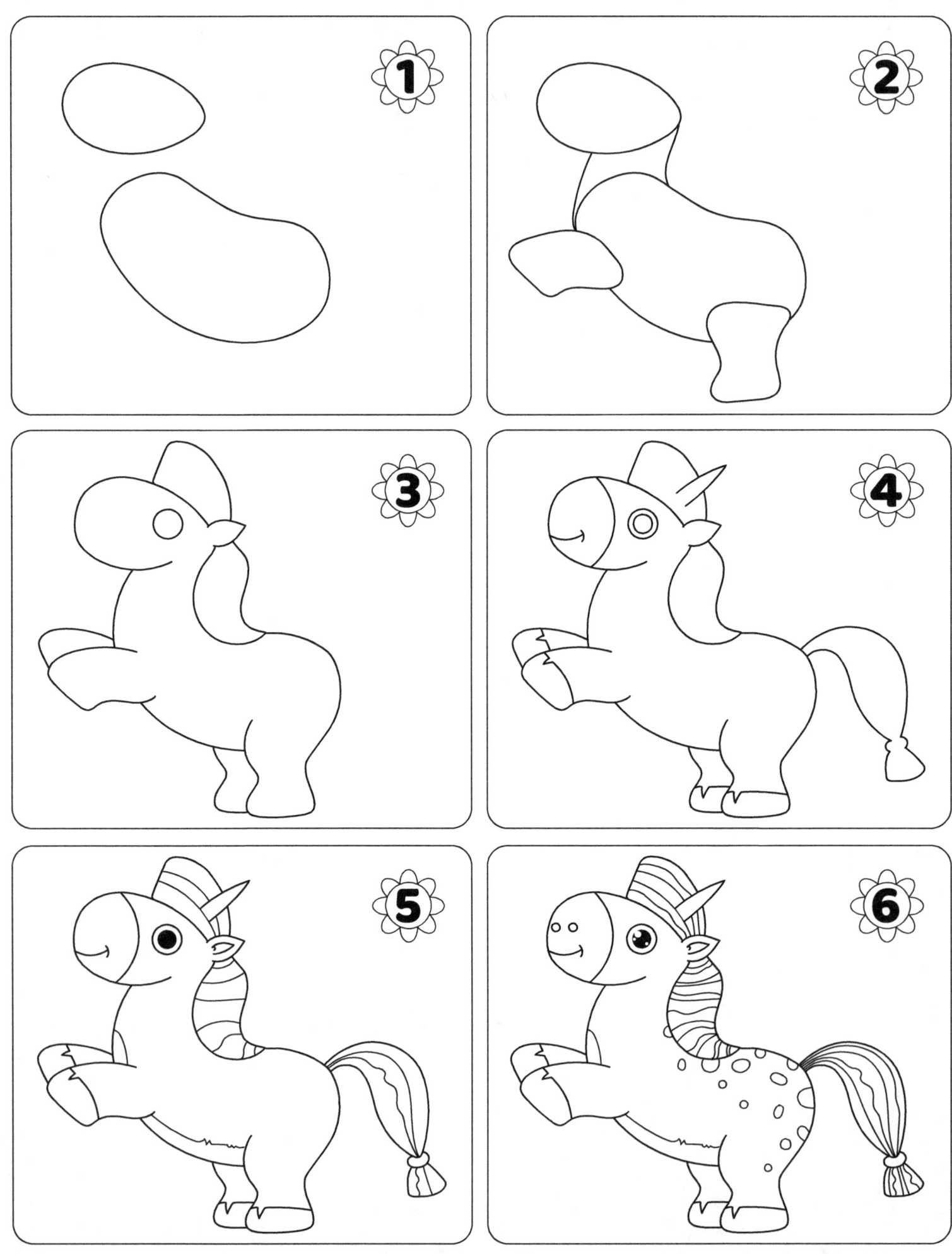

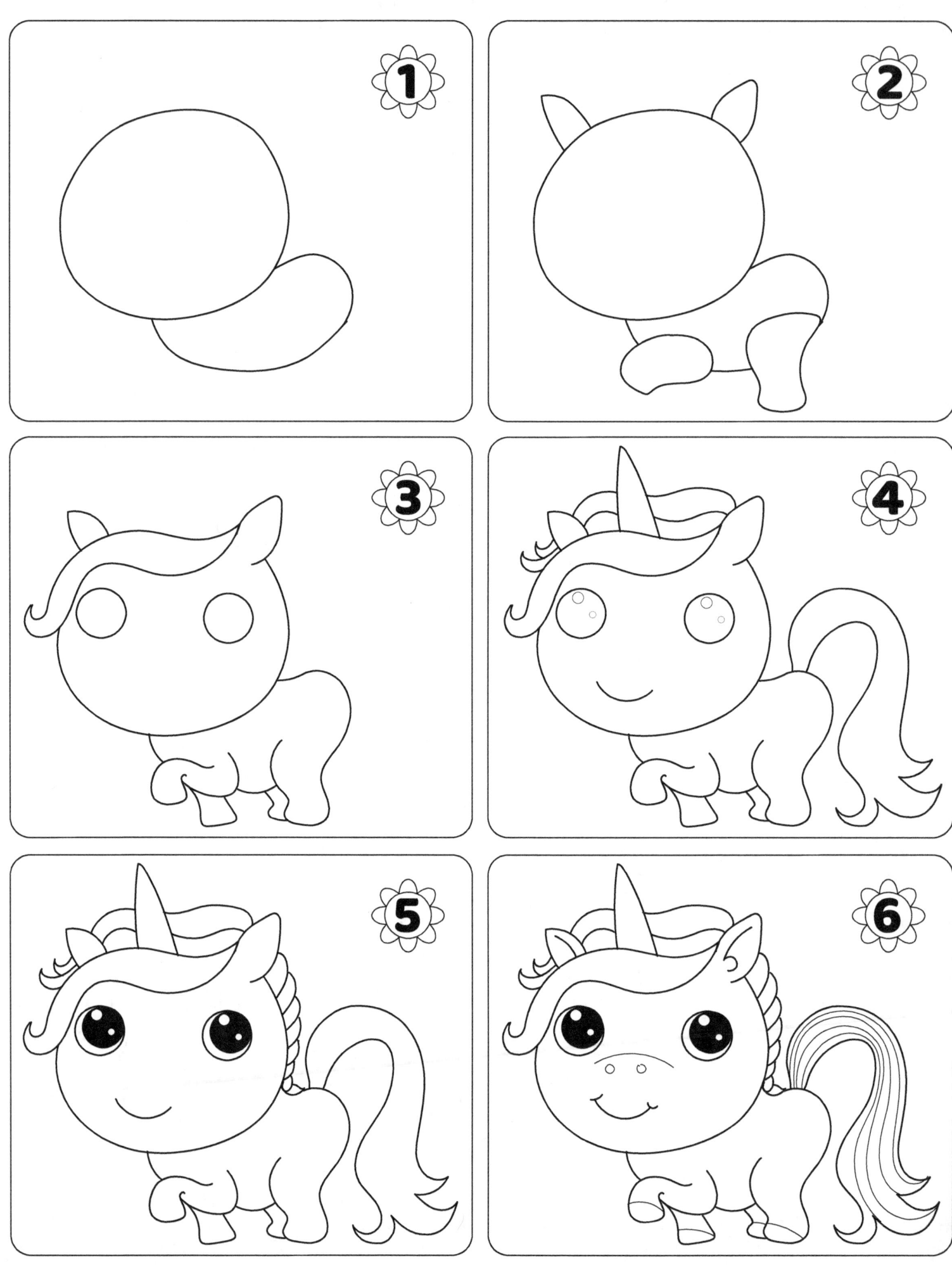

You Give It A Try!

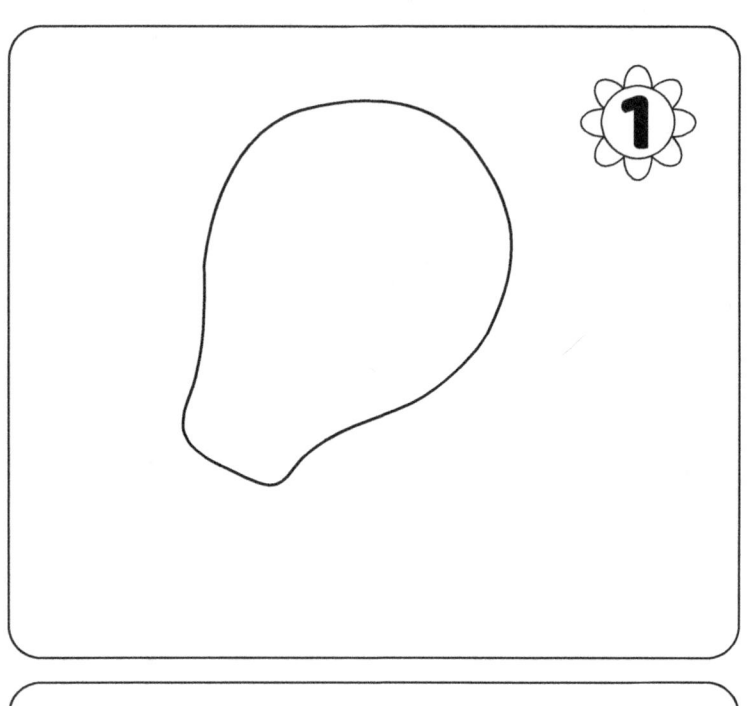

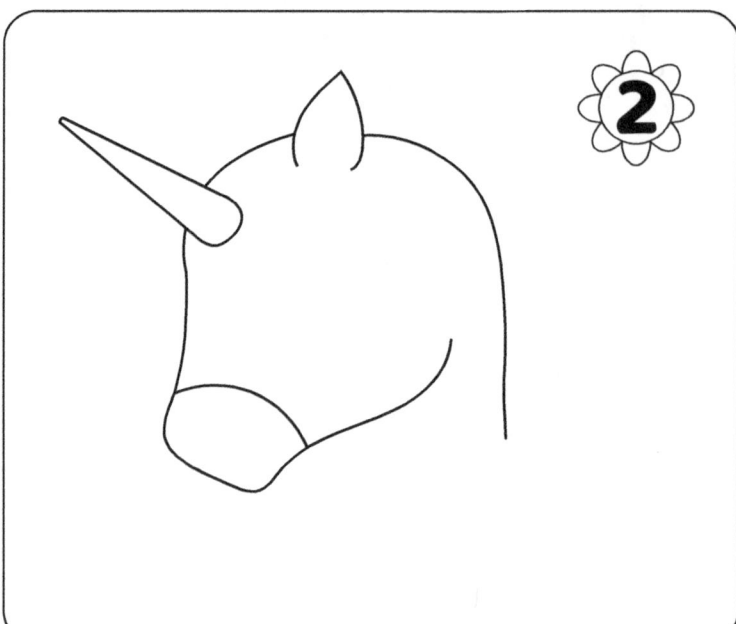

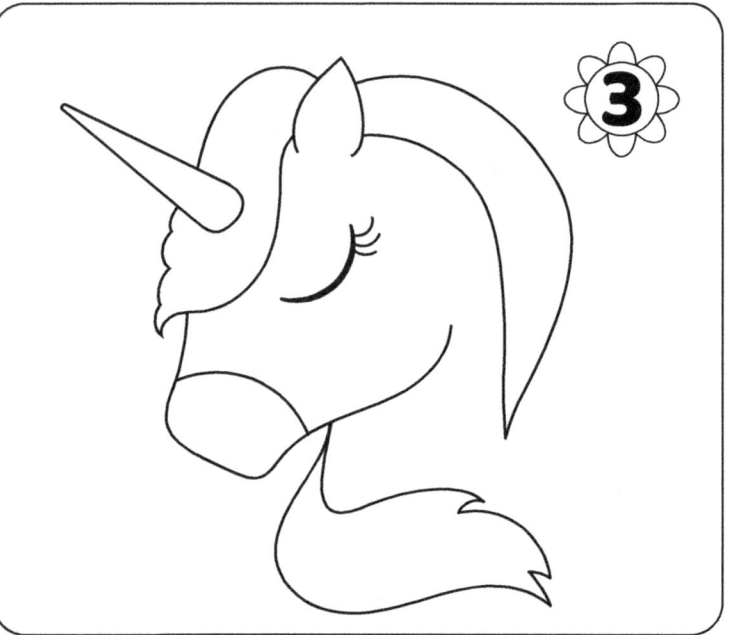

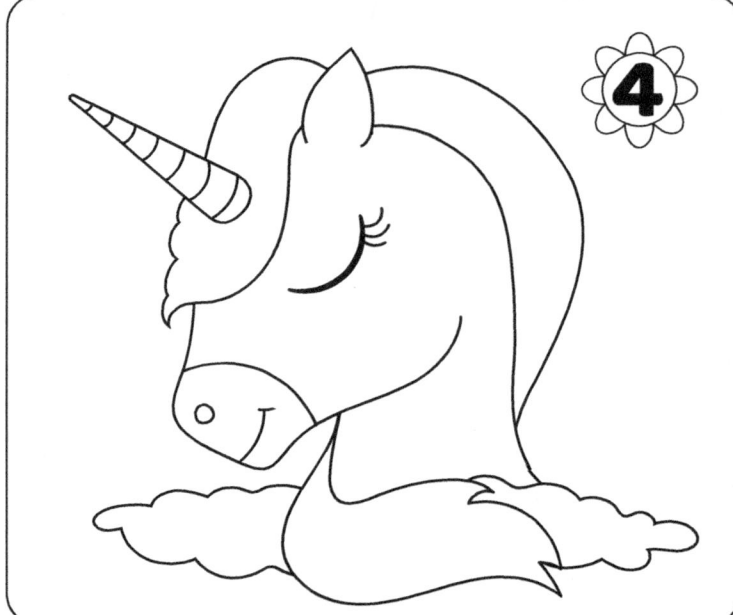

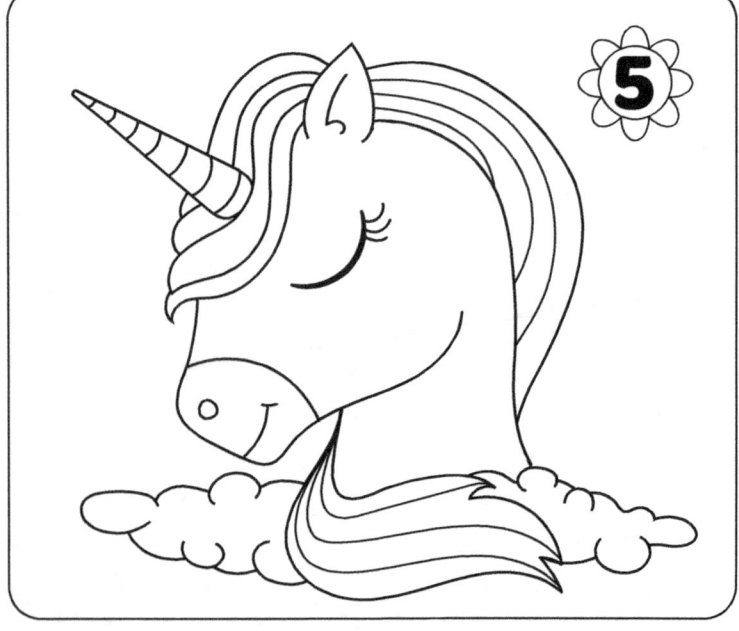

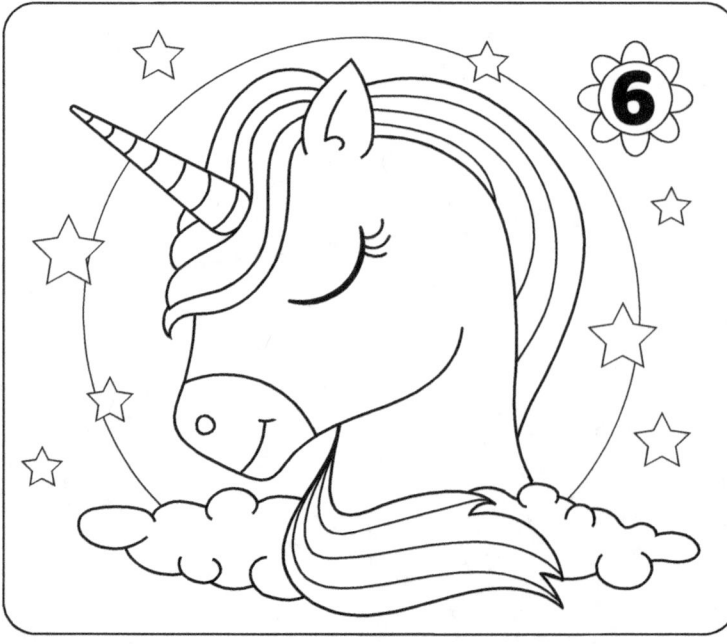

YOUR REVIEW

What if I told you that just one minute out of your life could bring joy and jubilation to everyone working at a kids art supplies company?
What am I yapping about? I'm talking about leaving this book a review.

I promise you, we take them **VERY seriously**.

Don't believe me?

Each time right after someone just like you leaves this book a review, a little siren goes off right here in our office. And when it does we all pump our fists with pure happiness.

A disco ball pops out of the ceiling, flashing lights come on... it's party time!

Roger, our marketing guy always and I mean always, starts flossing like a crazy person and keeps it up for awhile. He's pretty good at it. (It's a silly dance he does, not cleaning his teeth)

Sarah, our office manager runs outside and gives everyone up and down the street high fives. She's always out of breath when she comes back but it's worth it!

Our editors work up in the loft and when they hear the review siren, they all jump into the swirly slide and ride down into a giant pit of marshmallows where they roll around and make marshmallow angels. (It's a little weird, but tons of fun)

So reviews are a pretty big deal for us.

It means a lot and helps others just like you who also might enjoy this book, find it too.

You're the best!
From all of us goofballs at Big Dreams Art Supplies

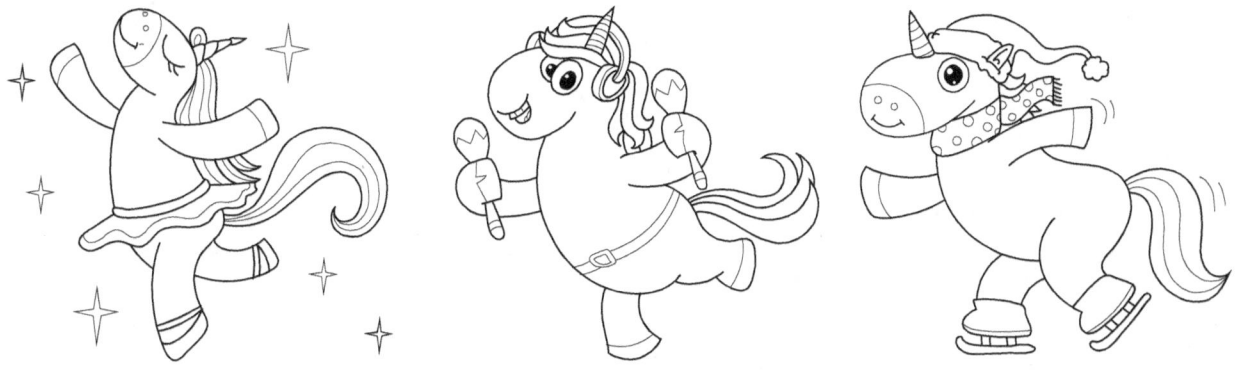